AMERICA'S
LAST CHANCE

AMERICA'S
LAST CHANCE

★ ★ ★ ★ ★

JEFF CROUERE

Cover and Interior Design: GKS Creative, Nashville

978-0-9972977-0-6 (Softcover)
978-0-9972977-1-3 (ePub)
978-0-9972977-2-0 (mobi)

Printed in the United States

FIRST EDITION

To the millions of Americans who have never lost faith in their country, who continue to participate in the political process by voting, donating, volunteering and running for elected office at all levels. May we return this government to these long suffering citizens, who have paid their taxes and their dues, but, in return, been neglected and abused by bureaucrats, lobbyists, special interest groups and corrupt politicians of both parties for so many years.

ACKNOWLEDGMENTS

Initially, I sincerely thank my friend and mentor, Antoinette Kuritz, for her expert guidance in showing an initial author how to complete the myriad steps necessary to finish and publish his first book. None of this would have been possible without her generous support.

Additional thanks to designer Gwyn Snider and editor Mark Clements for their valuable assistance on this project.

I want to thank all of the great listeners, viewers, supporters and sponsors of the Ringside Politics TV and radio programs. They have given me the inspiration to write this book and share my views on today's troubling political climate.

Thanks especially to the 17,000 guests who have graciously participated in my programs over my 17 years in the media. They have given me tremendous insights on countless issues and helped me clarify my positions on the pressing problems we face today.

None of this would have been possible without the backing of Chris Beary, Principal Owner, Richard Tate, General Manager, and the entire staff of WGSO 990 AM. Their steadfast encouragement of my program over the years has been crucial to any success I have been able to achieve.

In addition, much appreciation is also given to Ron Yager, WLAE-TV Vice President and General Manager and Jim Dotson, LAE Productions Vice President and General Manager, for their generous support of my television program.

No acknowledgment would be complete without thanking my mother for her tireless faith and devotion to my endeavors, my son Johnny and daughter Colette for their love and my wife Simone for inspiring me on a daily basis and instilling in me the confidence to complete this project.

And unending thanks to Almighty God for the countless blessings He has bestowed upon this nation throughout our history and the opportunity He has now afforded us to save the United States of America.

CONTENTS

I

"The Republicans frankly have been a disaster."
—Mark Meckler, Co-Founder of the Tea Party Patriots

INTRODUCTION

After years of losing to Democrats in presidential elections and seeing no concrete conservative reforms from the GOP Congress, the Republican Party faithful have had enough. As the country enters the 2016 election season, the GOP is in the midst of a revolution. The big money Political Action Committees no longer control the nomination process. Polls show that the Republican establishment candidates, despite spending massive amounts of money on advertising, are not winning—instead, conservative "outsiders" are taking the lead.

In the current election, the original favorite was former Florida Governor Jeb Bush, but he had a terrible start and shortly before this writing dropped out of the race. The two candidates who have done best so far are Donald Trump and Texas Senator Ted Cruz, both known as outsiders who are comfortable bucking GOP party leaders and causing them headaches.

This is the election that will either destroy the conventional Republican power base and turn the tables on the selfish insiders who have done so much harm to the GOP, or mark the end of the Republican Party as we know it—for good or for ill. True conservatives, those who believe in limited government, individual responsibility, free enterprise and protecting Constitutional rights, are sick and tired of being used and abused by the party so many of them have depended on to represent them in government.

If another moderate insider does get rammed through as the presidential nominee this July, millions of conservatives will show their disgust by either staying home in November or voting third party. Either way, after the election, a serious conservative third party movement could very well result.

If Republican leaders are smart, they will not try to circumvent the will of the majority of GOP voters, who so often are ignored. These are the activists, volunteers and small donors who are the lifeblood of the Republican Party. Sadly, Republican leaders have a history of making idiotic decisions and backing the wrong candidates. They are also infamous for thwarting conservative legislation and ignoring demands from their base.

This book highlights some of the inner Republican Party battles of the Obama years, and lays out the clear divisions that have stubbornly persisted within the GOP. It also plainly and repeatedly chronicles an important fact: *In the 2016 election, conservatism is the GOP's only path for victory*. It's time for the Republican Party to learn from its mistakes; if not, conservatives should leave the party and never come back.

As a former Executive Director and Deputy Chairman of the Louisiana Republican Party, I have followed local, state and national politics very closely. Too often I have noticed that the politically powerful ignore the wishes and needs of the grassroots. It seems that once power is achieved, politicians and party leaders become insular and non-responsive to the needs and demands of average Americans. This has resulted in a growing anger among the American people. First it was reflected in the Tea Party movement, and then, in the last year, by the rise of Donald Trump.

After almost two terms of Obama as President, more voters have become disgusted by a lack of action among politicians in both parties. Yet this anger is especially apparent in the Republican Party. Even though the GOP took control of both the House and Senate during portions of the Obama years, nothing of substance was accomplished. The demands of the voters were ignored. This lack of action has created the phenomenon of Donald Trump in this election.

I understand this feeling of disgust with GOP leadership because I have been hearing it from my callers since 1999, when I launched my Ringside Politics radio show. A year later I started a complimentary program, the Ringside Politics TV show. Through the years, I have interviewed 17,000 guests and talked to even more on the program who call in with their comments. One thing I understand clearly is that people want to save their country, but they want change. We cannot keep spending money we don't have, growing government, intruding on personal freedoms and shredding the Constitution. At some point very soon, unless we make a course correction we will reach a breaking point.

I wrote this book because I believe this election is our last chance to save the United States of America. If our country does not return to our traditional roots, reign in government, control our borders, and create meaningful jobs in America again, we may lose the country that Ronald Reagan referred to as that "Shining City upon a Hill." The stakes have never been higher and no election has ever been more important.

II

2009

No More Bushes

It did not take long for the Bush family to start touting Jeb for president. Even before George W. Bush had finished his term, former President George H. W. Bush told *Fox News* that his son Jeb would make a great president. According to the former president, Jeb was "as qualified and as able as anyone I know in the political scene."

Bush 41 said, "I'd like to see him (Jeb) run, I'd like to see him be president someday." The former president noted that Jeb Bush has a strong commitment to public service and that "as president, it's about service, service for the greatest country on the face of the Earth and the honor that goes with it. I think Jeb fits that description."

Jeb Bush might be the greatest guy in the world and the most capable public servant in American history, but the 2016 election made clear that the American people did not want him to be elected President of the United States. After two Bush presidencies and decades in public service for various family members, the country had been exposed to enough of the Bush family. Americans don't like dynasties, especially one that delivered two unsuccessful presidencies. George Bush 41 squandered the Reagan legacy, raised taxes and lost his bid for a second term. His son almost doubled the national debt, added government departments and entitlements, passed massive pork barrel government spending programs, and finished his term by bailing out Wall Street.

By the end of George W. Bush presidency, Americans had had their fill of the Bush family, giving "W" an anemic approval rating of only 22%, the lowest in the history of polling. Even George W. Bush's most ardent admirers admitted he had made serious errors during his terms as president. All of that baggage certainly carried over to Jeb Bush.

The 2008 elections should have been a wake-up call for Republicans, who had for too long been dominated by the Bush family, among other political insiders. Even former President George H. W. Bush realized the mood of the nation by admitting that it was probably a "bad time" for Jeb Bush to run for president because the country has had "enough Bushes in there."

Yes, indeed, George W. Bush tarnished the family name, and even though Jeb was a successful Governor of Florida, the country needs a breather before another Bush is elected President. In previous times it would have been impossible for a relative of Herbert Hoover, Richard Nixon or Jimmy Carter to be elected president; the same is the case with the Bush family, at least for the 2016 election.

Although the Bush family business has long been politics, for at least the next few years they need to find another line of work.

Conservatism Works if Tried

Americans fired the Republican Party in the 2006 and 2008 elections for good reasons. The George W. Bush years were very unkind to the party, which, led by the biggest spender of all time, moved away from the GOP's longstanding principles of individual responsibility, limited government, reduced taxes and the expansion of freedom.

If Republicans would follow through on their commitments, they could win a presidential election once again; their pro-liberty message is a great contrast to President Obama's horrible legacy of more government intervention and reckless spending.

The problem is that in the decades since Ronald Reagan left office, the GOP has been reluctant to follow true conservative principles. For example, in response to the financial crisis of 2008, President George W. Bush offered a number of bailout programs to Wall Street and the big banks. Yet Americans who lost over half of the value of their stock portfolios were never bailed out. The insiders and the elite won again, while average Americans were left holding an empty bag.

This predicament only intensified when President Obama took office, as he sought for the government to control every aspect of our lives. As evidence, we only need to look at Obamacare, or plans for climate change legislation, or the impediments to fossil fuel production in this country. These initiatives ignore the incompetence of government, and are certain to lead our country toward disasters of the sort seen in Greece and other European countries—examples that dramatically highlight how more government intervention leads to financial catastrophe.

Recovering from Bush Years

In the early days of the Obama administration, Republicans finally woke up from their Bush administration-induced coma and rediscovered their principles. On January 28, 2009, every House Republican cast the right vote and said *no* to the obscene spending bill offered by president Barack Obama. The so-called "stimulus bill" totaled $819 billion of mostly pork and useless spending.

This bill would only have added to our budget deficit and national debt, and thrown billions of dollars away on government programs designed to do nothing but increase the scope of the federal bureaucracy.

Unfortunately, during the first six years of the George W. Bush administration, when Republicans controlled the U.S. Congress, the party blew a great opportunity. These Republicans were complicit when President Bush turned a surplus into a deficit, added government departments, and created new entitlement programs. Bush was a fiscal disaster: the president who ushered in the financial catastrophe that still haunts the country. Sadly, Republicans did nothing to stop him. They did not demand a balanced budget or a reduction in the scope of government spending. The final insult was Bush's mad rush to pass the financial bailout package, a $750 billion boondoggle that was a gift for Wall Street at the expense of Main Street. From a big government Republican to a hard core liberal, the country has been electing presidents who have fallen further away from conservative principles.

Barack Obama also believes in the power of government to solve problems and rescue the economy. Unsurprisingly, his stimulus plan did not create jobs or solve our financial problems; instead it rewarded cronies and expanded the government. Although all House Republicans eventually recovered their spines and did the right thing, the party did not have enough votes to stop the stimulus package from passing.

It was during the Bush years that Republicans had the power to effect change. Instead, they succumbed to the power, prestige and the perks of office, and abandoned their constituents and principles to support a misguided president.

Only after Obama took office did Republicans finally start complaining about the size of government and poor fiscal policies, but by then it was too late to stop the president and his spending freight train.

Still, the vote against the stimulus package was beneficial because it sent a message to conservative Republicans across the country: the Reagan wing of the party was not dead after all. In fact, the stimulus vote represented the first of many battles in those years where Republicans opposed elements of the Obama agenda. But this was only the first step in the long journey conservatives must make if they want to stay relevant, save the GOP, and reconnect with disillusioned conservatives throughout the country.

Party Establishment Fights Conservatives

For years there has been a real schism between the GOP party establishment and the conservatives who make up the backbone of the party. A perfect example was revealed in March of 2009 when RNC Chairman Michael Steele went on a CNN show to describe talk show host Rush Limbaugh as "incendiary" and "ugly." The next day on his radio show, Limbaugh returned fire and told Steele that he was not a "pundit" and should concentrate on building the GOP. Of course the result was that Steele had to apologize. Over the next few weeks, several other GOP leaders attacked Limbaugh, but in each case they had to apologize after incurring the wrath of Limbaugh's legion of fans.

In fact, Limbaugh represented 20 million listeners, while Steele represented a party that had just lost the presidency and control of Congress. For decades, Limbaugh was the biggest force in talk radio, a successful broadcasting medium that reaches listeners disillusioned with the liberal mainstream media. In contrast, the Republican Party leadership was dreadful, losing both the 2006 mid-term election and the 2008 presidential election. One of the reasons for the debacle was that GOP nominee John McCain discarded tried and true conservative principles. For example, he supported the Wall Street bailout and was unable to clearly articulate a vision for America. He did not inspire the American people or educate them about the liberal agenda of Obama. Not surprisingly, millions of grassroots conservatives revolted and did not vote at all, while winnable Independent voters turned toward Barack Obama, helping ensure his victory.

Sadly, Steele is typical of the establishment wing of the Republican Party which, instead of focusing on overcoming the socialist agenda of the Democrats, prefers to wage an ugly war against conservatives like Rush Limbaugh. All Republicans should have united to challenge the Obama administration's agenda of higher taxes, more government, and marching toward socialism. Unfortunately, too many Republicans like Steele decided to bash their conservative colleagues instead of stopping the Obama spending machine.

Therefore, Republicans are partially responsible for the $8 trillion increase in the national debt that has occurred during the seven years of President Obama—especially since Republicans controlled the House of Representatives during four of those years, yet only made the spending problem worse.

Colin Powell, the Democrats' Favorite Republican

In May of 2009, the Republican darling of the media and the Democratic Party, former Secretary of State Colin Powell, was busy blasting the Republican Party for being too conservative. It was an ironic charge. Powell believed that after eight years of forgoing true conservative principles and embracing "compassionate conservatism," the party had become too right wing. How ridiculous!

George W. Bush and his administration created a massive increase in government spending, a doubling of the national debt, and the creation of new bureaucracies and entitlement programs. They tried to solve almost every problem with more spending and more government involvement. Bush never vetoed a spending bill, and left office with a budget deficit of almost $500 billion.

Of course this number only skyrocketed under Obama, but that does not excuse Bush's role in expanding the government. He inherited a budget surplus, yet squandered this opportunity to truly reform the federal government. He also seemed dedicated to involving government in even more areas of daily life. For example, he created "faith based" initiatives as a major part of his administration; however well-intentioned this program, the deeper spiritual problems facing America will never be solved by government. Most faith-filled believers look for answers in prayer and turning to God, not government.

After the debacle of Bush, Republicans should have embraced a genuine conservative alternative to the Democrats. Instead, in 2008 the GOP continued down the moderate path by nominating the media's favorite maverick, U.S. John McCain (R-AZ). During the campaign, McCain and Obama agreed on such key issues as global warming, campaign finance reform, and enhanced interrogation techniques, to name just a few. The results of the election were not surprising: McCain was slaughtered by a true liberal who stood to the left of the Arizona Senator on many issues.

These results confirm once again that when Republicans do not offer a stark contrast to Democrats, they lose. In recent years, Gerald Ford, Bob Dole, George H. W. Bush, McCain and Mitt Romney each lost the presidency while running as moderates.

However, when the Republican Party offers a true conservative alternative, it wins. For example, Ronald Reagan won a 44 state landslide in 1980 and a 49 state landslide in 1984 while running as a true conservative. Ten years later, the GOP took back control of Congress by using the Contract with America as a rallying point. This document was a set of conservative proposals intended to deal with the host of problems the government had created.

The problem was that Republicans, once in power, became just like Democrats. The GOP had a scanty record of reform during the Bush years. So, not surprisingly, in 2008 the people of this country voted to give the Democrats complete control, in effect punishing the GOP for ineffective leadership.

The Republicans should try conservatism *because it works*. In contrast, moderate policies that are nothing more than warmed-over liberal Democratic proposals never succeed. They only cost the GOP.

In the 2008 election, Secretary Powell voted for Barack Obama, overlooking exactly the type of moderate candidate he had often advocated for the Republican Party! McCain had decades of experience compared to Obama's inadequate resume. Clearly, it seems that Powell made his decision based on race and race alone. Unfortunately, millions of African Americans followed suit, and, helped elect to the White House the most liberal president in our country's history.

If the GOP follows Powell's advice and moves even more to the political center and left, it will soon cease to be a major political party, and a conservative third party will emerge. The only way for the Republicans to survive in 2016 and beyond is to embrace conservatism and offer a bold contrast to the Democrats. Let Powell, former Governor Tom Ridge, New York Congressman Peter King and a handful of other moderates leave the party. They are ideologically better suited to the Democratic Party on almost every issue.

The Republican Party needs to become a party of principle, offering reasoned criticism of the Democratic Party and its liberal ideology, as well as detailed conservative alternatives. In the process, the GOP needs to reconnect with the millions of people who sympathized with the Tea Parties and are upset at what is happening to our country today.

If the GOP does not tap into this brewing outrage, it will cease to serve any effective function and might as well cease to exist.

III

2010

Rise of the Tea Party

The elections of 2010 finally delivered real change to the country. One such earthquake occurred in May in the state of Kentucky, when the establishment GOP Senate candidate lost to the Tea Party's champion, Dr. Rand Paul. This was one of many examples of the grassroots power of the new movement. Dr. Paul was elected because he espoused core principles such as less government, lower taxes and the protection of personal liberty, which were articulated by so many Americans in the Tea Party movement.

By September, more Tea Party candidates had won GOP primaries in Kentucky, Nevada, Alaska, and a host of other states. The most shocking example occurred in Delaware where, despite a media onslaught against her, Tea Party candidate Christine O'Donnell easily defeated RINO (Republican in Name Only) Mike Castle in the Delaware Republican primary.

Unfortunately, these Tea Party victories were not the final nail in the political coffin of the establishment, which would live to fight another day. Still, by mid-2010 the grass roots in the Republican Party identified totally with the Tea Party movement. Conservatives were sick and tired of country club, establishment Republicans who offered watered-down liberalism and produced legislation only slightly better than that endorsed by liberal Democrats. When moderate Republicans are in the minority, they don't even try to stop nightmare pieces of legislation like Obamacare and executive decisions such as amnesty for illegal aliens.

O'Donnell's most vociferous opponent was GOP consultant Karl Rove, who did his best to create a negative image of her amongst Delaware voters. Rove hated O'Donnell because she was a Tea Party candidate. For years, he has been the poster boy of the establishment. While serving in the George W. Bush administration, he was the architect of the policies that expanded the government, produced massive budget deficits, created the TARP monstrosity, and failed to enforce border security. Under Rove and Bush, new government departments were created, entitlements established, massive earmark-laden bills passed . . . and the anger of the American public rose accordingly.

The Republican Party should have stopped listening to Karl Rove already, since he helped create the electoral debacles of 2006 and 2008. When he saw the Tea Party arise, he used his Fox News platform to attack Tea Party candidates as extremists and radicals.

Any loyal Republican should have been overjoyed, for the Tea Party movement was truly exciting. It represented this country's most consequential political movement in decades, where previously uninvolved citizens mobilized to take action and fight back against the establishment in both political parties.

Voters were angry at not only Obama Democrats, but Republicans as well; after all, it was the Country Club Republicans of the Bush administration who had created the high deficits and massive government programs in the first place. With the Tea Party, voters began listening to their hearts and voting with their pocketbooks. The Tea Party offered the GOP a road map to victory.

The Tea Party quickly became both powerful and popular. According to a Pulse Opinion Research poll, 52 percent of likely voters supported the Tea Party movement in September of 2010. This majority spelled victory against the forces of the status quo in *both* political parties.

Recent political history teaches us that Republicans are victorious only when they offer a stark contrast to the liberal policies of the Democratic Party. For example, when Ronald Reagan was nominated in 1980, the so-called experts predicted a massive defeat for the GOP. Instead, Reagan won in a landslide, followed by an even bigger landslide victory in 1984. Ten years later, the Contract with America was created. Skeptics claimed that it was too conservative, but instead of being defeated, Republicans won control of Congress for the first time in four decades.

By 2010, the Tea Party movement had gained a great deal of control over the Republican Party, but the empire had only begun to strike back. RINOs did not care that the country was in financial crisis or that their policies had contributed to the problem. Their solution was to grab for more political power—but first they had to remove the obstacle standing in their way: The Tea Party. The GOP establishment actually targeted the Tea Party more than they did their Democratic Party opposition!

Tea Party leaders realized they could not rest, even as they began winning primaries. Their primary goal was the complete takeover of the Republican Party; otherwise none of their other goals would ever get accomplished. Or, in the event the establishment took back control of the GOP, there was a second option: find a new political home.

Palin Powers Tea Party
to Electoral Success

In just 20 months, the Tea Party movement changed the face of politics in America. By 2010, citizens were ready to fire those responsible for the mess we were in; they were ready to try the Tea Party.

Former Alaska Governor Sarah Palin understood what was happening. She knew that a tidal wave of change was sweeping across America. In fact, Palin was one of the few real leaders of the Tea Party movement. She used her celebrity to help many of the Tea Party candidates running in Republican primaries. In the process she bucked the GOP establishment and created many enemies. Nevertheless, in almost every instance, Palin won, and the country club wing of the Republican Party lost. This success catapulted Palin to become an ever-bigger fundraising draw and a very popular figure in the party. Every GOP candidate wanted Palin to appear at their fundraiser.

As a result, Palin started testing the political waters for herself. In September of 2010 she appeared at a Reagan Dinner in Iowa, the home of the first caucus in the race for the 2012 Republican presidential nomination. While national polls showed that Palin trailed Mitt Romney, Mike Huckabee and Newt Gingrich, she was still a significant force within the party.

No other GOP leader had been as vocal as Palin in supporting the Tea Party movement. As a proud conservative, she did not deviate from her views in order to curry favor with the party establishment. No one else risked their political capital on so many Tea Party candidates as she did. Palin had the backbone to stand up to the media elite, the Republican Party establishment, and her critics. She represented a chance to overthrow the establishment and start fresh with a whole new lineup of leaders aligned with the Tea Party movement. She had accumulated political IOUs, power and success. There was no doubt that the old guard viewed her not as an ally, but as a threat.

2010 GOP Victories Due Only to the Tea Party

The elections of 2010 sent a clear message to the political establishment: Republicans should not feel too comfortable about their large margin of victory. Indeed, the GOP was placed on a very short leash. While voters repudiated the big government policies of President Obama, they did not want to return to the failed policies of Republican President George W. Bush, either. Elected Republicans risked a very short-lived reign of power if they did not deliver real results.

During the Bush years, when the RINOs were in charge and the federal government exploded in size, a budget surplus turned into $458 billion in deficits, the government added entitlement programs like Medicare prescription drugs, and social spending ballooned with impractical programs like "No Child Left Behind." In addition, a brand-new federal bureaucracy was created, the Department of Homeland Security.

The message of the 2010 election was that voters did not want big government solutions for our societal problems. Voters were motivated by the Tea Party lesson of a return to the bedrock Constitutional principles which made this nation great. They were also voting against the socialist agenda of Barack Obama and a Democrat-controlled Congress that had quadrupled the already large deficits of George W. Bush. They were voting against a party that had added more to the national debt in 21 months than the nation had accumulated in the previous forty presidential administrations, spanning two hundred years.

Obama had pushed so far to the left that the country naturally turned to the Republicans as a counterbalance to his agenda. Historically, the party out of power wins big in mid-term elections. In 1994, Republicans captured 52 House seats and took control of Congress for the first time since the Eisenhower years. Then, in 2006, Republicans lost control of Congress again as Democrats rode a wave of voter dissatisfaction with the Bush presidency. In the 2010 election things swung back the other way as voters sent a loud message repudiating the Obama agenda. The GOP picked up an amazing 63 seats in the House and six in the Senate.

Voters were stating that with the Democrats in control of Congress, the previous four years had been a nightmare for the country. House Speaker Nancy Pelosi was such a hated figure that "Fire Pelosi" rallies were held all across the country.

By the 2010 election, the country had been foundering in the worst economy since the Great Depression. Under Democratic leadership the stock market had fallen, trade and budget deficits had soared, unemployment had more than doubled, and a housing crisis was still gripping the nation.

After two years of Democrat Party control of Congress and the White House, the overwhelming majority of American voters were ready for the Republicans to take action to reduce the size of government, push for tax reduction and roll back the socialist programs of President Obama, especially the disastrous healthcare plan. In the mid-term election, voters were resending the message first proclaimed by Ronald Reagan in the 1970s: the Republican Party should enact conservative policies and raise "a banner of no pale pastels, but bold colors."

The 2010 election was a mandate for the Republican Party to fight President Obama on a range of important issues. It was an opportunity for the Tea Party to take control of the party away from the RINOs, who had had their chance for success and failed. Most importantly, it was an opportunity for the Tea Party to follow the timeless truths of the Founding Fathers and fight to save the country.

GOP Should Embrace Tea Party Principles

The principles of the Tea Party offer political salvation for the Republican Party. It was the Tea Party, after all, and not RINOs, who delivered the votes leading to the overwhelming Republican victories of 2010. Many establishment Republicans have more in common with Democrats than with Tea Party members. Because since 2010 RINOs have worked with Democrats, their ideological brethren, to increase deficit spending and erode Constitutional rights, they should have openly switched their allegiance to the Democratic Party. Instead, they fought against the rise of the Tea Party, and eventually regained control of all of the top GOP positions in Congress.

This path is not a formula for success for the Republican Party; for example, look at what happened to GOP presidential nominees Bob Dole, John McCain and Mitt Romney. After George H. W. Bush raised taxes, he lost the next election, and his son's big spending policies led to massive defeats in 2006 and 2008. The George W. Bush presidency was a RINO administration masquerading as a conservative one.

This country is at an important crossroads. We cannot continue to spend the inheritance of our children and grandchildren. A major course correction is needed; unfortunately, conservatives and Tea Party members are fighting not only the Democrats but the GOP establishment. In the 2016 election the conservative victory must be total and complete; otherwise, conservatives should find another political home.

IV

2011

Tea Party Stayed in GOP

When the Tea Party movement first began, some people wanted to see it organize into a separate political party. But eventually, most organizers decided to keep the Tea Party within the Republican Party in an attempt to force the GOP to return to Reagan-era conservatism. They failed, to the detriment of the party as a whole. If Republicans had stayed true to Tea Party principles, they would have energized the millions of grassroots supporters who originally became so involved in the movement.

One of the earliest supporters of the Tea Party was former Speaker of the House Newt Gingrich. As Speaker he served admirably in Congress and moved this country in the right direction with the Contract with America. By the time he finished his tenure as Speaker, the country enjoyed a budget surplus and Congress had passed both welfare reform and capital gains tax cuts.

However, after Gingrich left Congress, the country moved toward socialism regardless of whether leadership was Democrat or Republican. Therefore, both parties bear responsibility for today's fiscal mess and the fact that this country is in true peril. Gingrich, to his credit, listened to Tea Party leaders and took their advice to heart. With Tea Party encouragement, he jumped into the race for president in 2011, offering conservative proposals that contrasted clearly with the Obama agenda.

Unfortunately, the establishment of the Republican Party had other ideas. Instead of backing a conservative like Gingrich, who could have captured the support of the Tea Party movement, the establishment chose to support a 2008 retread, Mitt Romney. They wanted to crush the Tea Party movement and reassert control of the GOP. As noted by Sarah Palin, "Without the Tea Party there would have been no historic 2010 victory at all." The GOP owed its power to the Tea Party, but instead of showing thanks, it showed utter contempt.

Romney, a moderate who treated the Tea Party like the enemy, sealed the deal for Barack Obama, paving the way for his disastrous second term.

Obama Was Vulnerable Despite Bin Laden Raid

When Osama Bin Laden was killed, Obama-loving political pundits and liberal reporters loudly proclaimed how much the Navy SEAL operation helped the president in the polls.

One outlet, the Associated Press, even published a phony poll skewed to the Democratic side. It showed the president with an approval rating of over 60 percent. However, the poll respondents consisted mostly of Democrats, who were obviously supportive of Obama. Independent polls by Rasmussen, Gallup and others showed that Obama received at most a six percent jump in approval ratings after Bin Laden was killed. This did not compare favorably with the results for former President George W. Bush, who received a 35 percent boost in the polls after the 9/11 attacks and a 15 percent approval rating increase after Saddam Hussein was captured. Even worse for Obama, his approval rating dropped in the weeks following the raid.

With such tepid statistics, it was ludicrous for the Obama-loving media to tout the President as such a success. Of course, common sense and reality never matter for media liberals, who try to help the president in any way possible. Despite the popular Bin Laden raid, the fundamentals of the economy were still poor, so the President's poll numbers did not improve. Unfortunately for Obama supporters, no amount of media spin could change the fiscal reality for the American people.

This provided a real opportunity for Republicans, as economic conditions always seem to have a great impact on presidential elections. In fact, almost all presidential elections are decided on pocketbook issues. Back in 1992, Democratic analyst James Carville declared that "It's the Economy, Stupid." Carville's candidate, Bill Clinton, defeated a Republican incumbent who had enjoyed a 90 percent approval rating the previous year due to the successful conclusion of the first Gulf War. The election was decided on economic issues, not a successful military operation. What was true in 1992 was still true in 2011.

At that time, three years into Obama's first term, 40 different economic criteria showed that the country was in worse shape than it had been before the election. History teaches that no president has ever won re-election when the unemployment rate exceeds 7.5 percent, and in May of 2011, the unemployment rate was 9.0 percent. Millions of Americans were so disgusted that they simply stopped looking for work.

President Reagan's famous question posed in the 1980 debate against Jimmy Carter— "Are you better off today than you were four years ago?"—could have been used quite effectively by Republicans in the 2012 election. Most Americans were much worse off after a few years of the Obama presidency. In fact, some analysts believe that Obama has been so ineffective that he qualifies as the worst president in U.S. history, wrenching the title away from the hapless Jimmy Carter.

In 2012 the Republican nominee had a large number of juicy issues to address with the American people, including continual budget deficits, mounting national debt, socialized medicine, skyrocketing gasoline prices, higher unemployment and renewed inflation. To win, Republicans had only to follow an easy plan: nominate a real conservative who would present a sharp alternative to Obama. Rather than a moderate like Ford, Dole or McCain, a conservative in the mold of Ronald Reagan stood the best chance of beating Obama and moving the country in the right direction.

A real conservative could have tapped into the growing Tea Party movement, which needed to be remobilized and reenergized for the 2012 election. Only a real conservative could have excited the formidable Tea Party grassroots coalition and motivated the base of the party to vote. Instead, party insiders continued their push for their dream candidate, former Massachusetts Governor Mitt Romney, who was anathema to the conservative base.

CNN: An Improper Media Forum for GOP Debate

On June 14, 2011, seven GOP presidential candidates appeared in the second debate of the presidential campaign. While it was understandable that candidates would want to participate in a debate held in the first primary state of New Hampshire, it made no sense that they would agree to appear on CNN.

This network had earned the nickname "Clinton News Network" for boosting "Slick Willy" during his impeachment scandal, and is also known as the "Communist News Network" because its founder, Ted Turner, is a radical leftist who is quite sympathetic to dictators and enemies of the United States.

The shows that aired on CNN during this time were all hosted by liberals: John King, Wolf Blitzer, Elliot Spitzer, Piers Morgan, and Anderson Cooper. The network did not have a single conservative host on its schedule. In fact, CNN fired Spitzer's moderate co-host and gave the entire show to the disgraced Democratic politician best known for being a hooker's "Client Number Nine." The so-called conservatives used by CNN as analysts were all very moderate or unimpressive. The deck was stacked severely to the far left.

The seven Republican candidates should have declined to appear on such a biased network, but the debate went on. Not surprisingly, the format was ridiculous, with moderator John King interjecting annoying grunts and trying repeatedly to cut off the comments of the candidates. He asked silly and inappropriate questions about late night comedians, TV shows, musicians, soft drinks, pizza and whether a candidate preferred "spicy or mild." In an attempt to invoke humor, King sidetracked the debate from the important issue of the horrible economy which was on the minds of almost all Americans.

The format also tried to play "Gotcha" with the candidates by tricking them on issues such as gay marriage and the military's "don't ask, don't tell" policy. These issues are important to only a fraction of GOP voters and should not have been included in a televised debate. Obviously, the goal of CNN was not to educate voters on important issues, but to embarrass Republican candidates.

Notwithstanding the unfortunate decision to appear on CNN, none of the candidates made any major mistakes. Of the seven, Newt Gingrich and Rick Santorum seemed to give the sharpest answers and connect best with the audience. Herman Cain was not at the top of his game, while Mitt Romney benefited because the other candidates refused to attack his healthcare plan or his numerous flip-flops on the issues.

Overall, the debate was trivial, focusing on unimportant issues, and broadcast on a network strongly tilted to the left. This was a perfect indication of how the Republican Party was trying to win the favor of the liberal media rather than satisfy the concerns of the conservative base.

The Rodney Dangerfield of American Politics

Comedian Rodney Dangerfield used to say, "I get no respect at all." It was his signature joke, a great punch line in his stand-up routines. Now that Rodney has graduated to the great comedy club in the sky, his "no respect" line should be adopted by another well-known personality, Ron Paul.

Prior to the 2012 election this Republican presidential

candidate almost always won straw polls, drew crowds of enthusiastic supporters, and had a rock star-like following. Paul was a hero to Americans who support limited government, the pursuit of personal liberty, and tried-and-true Constitutional principles.

Unlike GOP frontrunner Mitt Romney, Paul had consistently advocated these positions for the prior thirty years. His record in Congress had been steadfastly against the growth of government spending, federal regulation and increased taxes.

Unfortunately, due to his beliefs about allowing states to legalize drugs and pursuing a policy of military nonintervention, most mainstream news reporters and political analysts discounted his chances of winning the nomination. They claimed that no candidate with such "radical" views would be nominated by a party that supported the war on terror and the war on drugs.

However, Republican voters were not listening to the "experts." Despite rough media treatment, Paul raised more campaign donations for his 2012 campaign than he had in the 2008 race for president. This was a remarkable feat, considering that he was in his late 70s. In a media age of blow-dried Ken dolls like Romney, Paul was refreshingly different and real. Voters did not mind his wrinkles and gray hair. In the presidential polls of September 2011, Paul ran a strong third behind Mitt Romney and Texas Governor Rick Perry. In one such poll, conducted by CNN/ORC International, Paul placed third with an impressive level of 13 percent support.

Given this, the media should have highlighted Paul's recent achievements and touted him as a strong presidential contender. Instead, he was ignored and given no respect by the so-called opinion makers, who were intent on discounting him and publicizing Romney and Perry as the frontrunners.

Informed voters knew that Romney had a history of

changing his political positions when convenient, and that Perry was a former Democrat who had chaired the 1988 presidential campaign for Al Gore in Texas. Although Perry switched his party affiliation in 1989, he continued to advocate questionable views on border security and was a proponent of bestowing taxpayer benefits to illegal aliens. Similarly, while Governor Perry would later admit that his executive order mandating HPV vaccines for young girls was a mistake, it was troubling that he initially supported such government intrusion into what should have been a personal family matter.

Unlike Perry and Romney, Paul had been a model of consistency for decades. Everyone knew he supported sound monetary policy, a return to the gold standard, an audit of the Federal Reserve, real spending cuts, and true tax reform. This consistency was comforting to voters, who did not need to wonder where Paul stood on the issues. These bold positions highlighted the differences between the Libertarian Paul and most Republican elected officials, who change their positions with the shifting political winds.

Despite the label of "Libertarian," on most of the core issues Paul was in line with the rank and file voters in the Republican Party. His challenge was to break through the media wall of opposition and convince skeptical Republican insiders that he had a chance to win the election.

In contrast, Romney was a mushy moderate, and Perry a warmed-over Democrat who had converted to conservatism out of convenience rather than conviction.

Cain Inflicts Pain on RINOS and Black Liberals

After a strong showing in the Florida straw poll, businessman Herman Cain found his presidential candidacy on fire. In the October 2011 Gallup poll he was virtually tied with Mitt Romney for the lead among GOP presidential contenders.

For months Cain had performed well in debates, yet always languished near the bottom of the pack among Republican candidates. But after he performed exceptionally well in the televised debate held in Florida, he received renewed attention and support, built momentum and scored a massive win in the state's straw poll.

Once Cain won Florida, his national support climbed steadily and he started getting renewed attention from the national news media. Unfortunately, much of the coverage was nasty. Cain had to endure being called a racist and a draft dodger by Lawrence O'Donnell of MSNBC—who, incidentally, had received a deferment during the Vietnam War. O'Donnell questioned why Cain received a college education and worked as a ballistics expert for the U.S. Navy instead of joining civil rights protests and signing up for military service. The bottom line was that Cain admirably served his country, and O'Donnell looked foolish in trying to tarnish Cain's record.

The attacks intensified among the "lame stream" media, which dredged up radical black professor Cornel West and communist sympathizer Harry Belafonte to criticize Cain. West said that Cain had a "coldness toward poor people" while Belafonte called him a "bad apple." In response, Cain said he'd left the "Democratic plantation a long time ago" and the personal attacks "simply won't work."

As a conservative African American, Cain was especially scary to liberals in the media, Democratic Party and GOP. Unfortunately, the attacks on him only got worse as the media tried to replicate its treatment of other conservatives such as Sarah Palin and Michelle Bachmann. Sadly, this effort had the full support of establishment Republicans, who were backing Mitt Romney.

Although the RINOs loved Romney, his liberal past made him persona non grata to the Tea Party movement. Furthermore, Romney had flip-flopped his position on everything from his socialized medicine plan to abortion to global warming. In a Senate debate in Massachusetts he blasted Ronald Reagan, and admitted that he had been an Independent during the 1980s.

In contrast, Cain was a solid conservative who had had a consistent record for many years of speaking out on issues. He also had a very impressive background, having worked with the U.S. Navy, turned around Godfather's Pizza, and served as a talk radio host. Unlike Romney, who had been "born with a silver spoon in his mouth," Cain was a self-made man.

Cain was a unique candidate because, also unlike Romney, he had not been running for president for the past five years. He had been earning an income, working and prospering even during a very poor economy. He understood the plight of average Americans who were out of work and hoping for better economic conditions. These Americans wanted real solutions, not phony "hope and change" nonsense. Cain's "9-9-9" tax reform plan was an ingenious combination of the flat and fair tax plans that offered a radical change to the corrupt and oppressive tax system that stymied economic growth in the country. This tax plan was one of the major reasons Cain surged in the polls.

Along with giving real hope to struggling Americans, Cain's candidacy offered the potential of radically changing the electoral dynamics in our country. As a conservative African American, he would have made history had he become the first black Republican presidential nominee.

Cain felt he had a clear road to victory because he could attract as much as 33 percent of the black vote in the presidential race. This would represent a higher percentage of black votes than any GOP presidential candidate had received since the 1950s. In addition, Cain was a favorite of the Tea Party movement, a fact that dispelled the ridiculous notion that the grass roots phenomenon was populated by angry racists.

As the Republican nominee, Cain could have attracted a large and diverse coalition of voters to defeat the socialist agenda of Barack Obama. However, before he would even have a chance to face Obama he would have to defeat the Republican establishment's candidate, Mitt Romney, and win the nomination.

Conservatives knew that only a candidate like Cain could prevent them from having to "hold their nose" and vote for whoever else the GOP candidate might be. He would give the party a principled nominee, and Americans a real choice. But the question remained: Would the Republican Party finally nominate a candidate that conservatives could get excited about?

Of course not!

Herman Cain's High-Tech Lynching

The "lame stream" news media in this country is despicable, never failing to act as a willing accomplice of the liberals in the Republican and Democratic parties. Studies by Robert Lichter and others have shown that the vast majority of individuals in the mainstream news media vote for liberal candidates and support liberal positions. Lichter showed that in every presidential election since 1964, more than 81 percent of the media "elite" voted for the Democratic presidential nominee. Even in years of Republican landslides, such as 1972, almost all members of the media voted for the Democrat presidential candidate.

Naturally, these voting patterns lead to liberally-biased news coverage. What was true in 1972 was especially true in 2012 among the media elite based on the East Coast. Even with countervailing efforts on talk radio and the Internet and thousands of smaller news sites, the media elite still drove the coverage of political issues.

This bias was apparent whenever a liberal Democrat became involved in a scandal. In such cases the media rushed in to support the candidate. For example, even though the liberal media spent years covering for former president Bill Clinton, it was the conservative website the Drudge Report that exposed the Monica Lewinsky scandal. After the incident was revealed, big media was forced to follow. Later it was discovered that *Newsweek* magazine had known about Clinton's relationship with Lewinsky, but held up the story.

The whole impeachment saga was one in which the media blamed Republicans for dragging the country through the process, and Bill Clinton was exonerated. The media gave him a pass even though he had also been accused of rape by Juanita Broaddrick, sexual assault by Kathleen Willey, and sexual harassment by Paula Jones. He had lied about his sexual relationships with Gennifer Flowers and Monica Lewinsky, and in the process committed perjury and misled the American people, yet somehow the Republicans were the villains of the tale.

During the Clinton scandals, the media constantly defended the president and accused the various women of being "bimbos" or worse. Instead of praising them for having the courage to come forward, the media treated Clinton's accusers with disdain.

The same type of media behavior was on display whenever a liberal was charged with a sexual offense. In 2010, a massage therapist claimed that former Vice president Al Gore had sexually assaulted her. In fact, she referred to the Nobel Prize winning blowhard as a "sex crazed poodle." The media yawned and tried to destroy the reputation of the massage therapist.

Former Democratic presidential candidate John Edwards lied about an affair and a love child with a campaign staffer—a relationship that took place while his wife was dying of cancer. The major media was uninterested in the reports; only the investigative work of the *National Enquirer* shamed the rest of the media into covering the story. Edwards was eventually indicted on six charges involving his use of campaign funds to hide an affair with a videographer. He escaped prison only because the jury deadlocked on five counts of violating federal campaign contribution laws.

Similarly, unlike their treatment of liberals, the media attacked Herman Cain from the very beginning of his campaign. They tried to destroy him, mainly because he was a conservative African American rising in the polls. One method of media attack was to lampoon him as an idiot. For example, Martin Bashir of MSNBC wondered whether Cain knew "how to spell Iraq." As a dynamic communicator and successful businessman, Cain was clearly a threat to the GOP establishment and to the monolithic hold the Democratic Party always has on the black vote. In the end, he had to be destroyed.

Unlike John Edwards, Cain had not been charged with breaking any laws or financial misconduct. Unlike Clinton and Gore, he had never been charged with sexual assault. However, many years prior to his campaign, the National Restaurant Association had made a payment to at least one woman who alleged that Cain committed some sort of sexual harassment against her. Two other women alleged inappropriate behavior by Cain when he had served as an executive with the National Restaurant Association.

Despite confidentiality agreements, the media went into overdrive on these stories, trying to torpedo Cain's chances for the nomination. Compared to what Bill Clinton had been accused of doing, Cain's alleged behavior was mild. In essence, Cain was accused of making inappropriate comments and physical gestures. In other words, it might have been a misdemeanor in the world of sexual harassment, but certainly not a felony.

The wall-to-wall media coverage highlighted political analysts who blasted Cain for not being more forthcoming, even though the supposed behavior had occurred many years earlier. Any person would have a hard time remembering the exact circumstances of something that had occurred in the 1990's, but the media never gave Cain the benefit of the doubt. He was guilty until proven innocent, the opposite of the standard applied to Bill Clinton.

Sadly, the American people were played for fools once again by the liberal media. After initially ignoring the attacks on Cain and increasing their contributions to his campaign, people began to leave his campaign in droves. The all-out media assault had worked.

This case was reminiscent of the "high-tech lynching" in 1991 when conservative Supreme Court nominee Clarence Thomas had to undergo aggressive examination from Democrats and the media over ridiculous sexual harassment charges from Anita Hill. In the end, Ms. Hill did not claim rape, assault or any inappropriate touching, but something about a pubic hair on a can of Coke, and a reference to a porn actor.

Like Cain, Thomas was targeted because he was a conservative black man. Although Thomas survived to become a great Supreme Court Justice, Herman Cain was not so lucky.

Cain Train Derailed

The drumbeat of revelations eventually doomed Herman Cain's unconventional quest for the presidency. The last straw landed when a woman named Ginger White stepped forward to allege a 13-year affair with Cain. Whether she was telling the truth or not did not matter, the political damage was too great.

In the final weeks of his campaign Cain's donors lost faith in him, and without funds he was unable to continue in the race. Even before the Ginger White revelation, Cain had been dropping in the national polls, but he slipped from first place to third after four women accused him of sexual harassment.

The harassment claims were not very believable, since they involved supposed conduct from the 1990s, and one of the women was represented by the liberal attorney and infamous publicity hound Gloria Allred. However, the accusations of an affair carried more weight. Ms. White produced cell phone records showing 61 calls and text messages both to and from Herman Cain in the previous few months. The calls were made at various hours of the day and night to his private cell phone. When contacted, Cain admitted a relationship with Ms. White, but claimed it was just a friendship. If so, it must have been an unusually close one.

Ms. White was financially destitute, unemployed, and had just been evicted from her apartment. Despite these problems, she did not cash in on the accusations and was not paid by the Fox News affiliate in Atlanta that broke the story.

Ms. White said she had been forced to come forward because other media outlets were getting close to reporting the affair. A mother of two, she had filed a sexual harassment complaint against her boss in 2001 and had been successfully sued by an ex-business partner. All of this raised questions about her story, but the doubts were not strong enough to help Cain weather the storm, especially since he admitted to sending White money and not telling his wife about the arrangement. Along with the accusations of sexual harassment, it was all too much for the Herman Cain presidential campaign to survive.

The news disappointed his many supporters, who had enjoyed his unusual approach to the issues. To address our nation's problems, Cain offered fresh solutions rooted in his years as a business executive. His 9-9-9 tax reform plan was popular, but the personal controversies surrounding him eventually drowned out any news coverage of his reform ideas.

As Cain bowed out of the race, his conservative supporters dispersed amongst the other candidates. All this happened with the Iowa caucus just a few weeks away, always a crunch time for GOP presidential candidates. Herman Cain's train had run off the tracks before the first vote was even cast.

Multiple Choice Mitt in Meltdown

It all happened so suddenly for Mitt Romney. In early 2011 he was a strong frontrunner in the GOP race for president. In fact, most political analysts and media commentators were ready to award Romney with the nomination. But by late fall of 2011, Romney had gone into freefall. By the end of November 2011, a Rasmussen national poll showed former House Speaker Newt Gingrich with a 38-17 percent lead over Romney, the largest lead in the race to date. Gingrich was challenging Romney in New Hampshire and leading in the key early states of Iowa, Florida and South Carolina. Gingrich was connecting with voters and espousing a more conservative platform than Romney or the other candidates. He also had a successful track record as House Speaker that impressed Republican voters, especially in contrast with the current GOP leadership.

From the beginning of the 2012 race, conservatives had been

looking for an alternative to the moderate flip-flopper Romney. When former Alaska Governor Sarah Palin decided not to run, there was a stampede of support for Minnesota Congresswoman Michele Bachmann. After some unimpressive debate performances and television interviews, Bachmann's star dimmed and Texas Governor Rick Perry became the "hot" candidate—but then he bombed in numerous debates, and conservatives abandoned him in favor of Herman Cain, whose problems we've already described.

In the meantime, House Speaker Newt Gingrich kept moving up in the polls, buoyed by his strong debate performances and the troubles of the other conservative candidates. Although he had plenty of personal and political baggage of his own, his strong intellect and innovative ideas were catching fire with the conservative base of the Republican Party.

In contrast, Mitt Romney was seen as a tired old political opportunist who had been running continuously for president for five years. He had been on every side of almost every issue. Conservatives wanted a candidate they could trust, one with a proven track record promoting principles such as limited government and lower taxes.

Unfortunately, Romney sported a track record of liberalism in Massachusetts. As the Democratic National Committee exposed in an on-line video, "Mitt vs. Mitt," Romney had changed his position on the stimulus bill, abortion, Ronald Reagan, health care, unions, TARP, auto bailouts, immigration, global warming and assault weapons. He was clearly incapable of maintaining his position on almost any issue. In a 1994 U.S. Senate debate, the incumbent Ted Kennedy famously called Romney "not pro-choice, but multiple choice." For once, Ted Kennedy was 100 percent correct, and his characterization of Romney was especially true during the primary battle of 2011.

With all this bad news, Romney started to lose his cool. He accused Brett Baier of Fox News of asking "overly aggressive" questions, although the anchor was simply trying to get Romney to explain his ever-shifting positions on issues.

Clearly, the reason Romney had had to flip-flop so often was that he was the governor of the most liberal state in the nation. In 1988, the last time a Massachusetts governor had been nominated for president, things had not turned out too well. Democrat Michael Dukakis was destroyed by a rather unimpressive Republican nominee named George H. W. Bush.

In the 2012 race, conservatives were looking for a nominee with a consistent track record, the right principles, and the ability to handle a debate against an accomplished television performer, Barack Obama.

The last thing the Republican Party needed was a candidate who became flustered when asked tough questions.

V

2012

Once Again, the Country Club vs. the Tea Party

By early December of 2011, the moderate insiders in the Republican Party were not happy. Their favorite candidate, Multiple Choice Mitt Romney, was not doing too well in the polls. He was stuck in the 25 percent range and seemed to be unable to generate new support. Along the way, a host of conservative alternatives had passed him by, reflecting the clear distaste for Romney among the conservative base of the GOP.

This type of divide has been apparent in the Republican Party for over 50 years. The primary battles between Rockefeller vs. Goldwater, Ford vs. Reagan, Bush Sr. vs. Reagan, Dole vs. Forbes, and finally McCain vs. Huckabee exposed this ideological chasm.

Usually, the tired old insider country club wing of the Republican Party prevailed in these battles at the expense of the conservative grassroots. After all, insiders have access to big business and big money, while grassroots candidates have to rely on the popularity of their ideas. Still, the conservative base of the GOP occasionally wins. It happened in 1964 with Barry Goldwater, and in 1980 with Ronald Reagan. Unfortunately, it has not happened since, for the powerful Country Club wing of the party views conservatives not as fellow Republicans, but as threats to their power base. The elites do not want to relinquish their party positions to the grassroots, but they do want to retain their connections to the levers of power in the federal government. Unlike conservatives, who want to drastically reduce the size of government, most establishment Republicans want only to do a better job of managing the growth.

But in the 2012 election there was a different dynamic in play: the conservative wing had been energized by the Tea Party movement and was unwilling to shut up and accept a force-fed moderate flip-flopper like Mitt Romney as its nominee.

These true conservatives never warmed to Multiple Choice Mitt. In his previous life as a Massachusetts moderate, Romney had expressed support for abortion rights and the man-made global warming hoax, beliefs that should have been enough to disqualify him from the GOP nomination. On the other hand, Romney had lined up so many GOP insiders and big money supporters that he had a unique ability to overcome his handicaps. Would the grassroots base of the GOP buy the "new" Romney?

Initially, the conservatives who dominate the base of the GOP looked desperately for an alternative to Romney. They churned through a long list of potential nominees: Trump, Palin, Bachmann, Perry, Cain. By December of 2011, it was Newt Gingrich's turn at the top. He had more conservative credentials than the others and stood a better chance of winning the nomination. Unlike the other prospective conservative standard bearers, Newt was a recognized conservative icon with a 40-year record of activism.

Although he had made mistakes as Speaker of the House, he had also led the GOP to their first majority in 40 years. He had been at the helm when welfare reform, capital gains tax cuts, and a budget surplus were achieved. While his personal and ethical lapses had eventually caused his undoing, he'd used his time in the political wilderness to mature as a leader. By the time of the 2012 race, Gingrich was a changed man who had learned from his many mistakes. The new Newt was a devout Catholic with a stable marriage. No one could deny his intellectual brilliance. His performance in the debates was outstanding.

Of course, during his 40-year career Newt had made some ridiculous comments and more than a few mistakes, such as doing a television commercial with Nancy Pelosi. Yet he was a true conservative, with a lifetime American Conservative Union voting record of 90 percent. Without Gingrich there would have been no Republican house majority for the first time in 40 years, no budget surplus, no welfare reform, no 11 million new jobs and no capital gains tax cuts. He drove both the Republicans to power in the House of Representatives and the Clinton administration to the right. Without Gingrich, Bill Clinton would have unleashed a strident liberal agenda on the American people—a very frightening thought.

As soon as conservative voters recognized Gingrich's attributes, they started to move to his campaign in droves. Meanwhile, the RINO brigade—composed of Washington D.C. insiders, consultants, bundlers, two-bit talking heads, and the country club set—grew frenzied. Their mission: destroy Newt.

At first, the more they criticized him, the better his poll numbers grew. As Peggy Noonan explained, "The antipathy of the establishment not only is not hurting him at this early date, it may be helping him. It may be part of the secret of his rise. Because establishments, especially the Washington establishment, famously count for little with the Republican base: 'You're the ones who got us into this mess.'"

Amen! The grassroots base of the GOP knew quite well that big spending Republicans were just as bad as liberal Democrats.

Both groups had caused the horrific problems facing the country.

By December 2011 the remaining Republican candidates for president had divided into three groups. The moderate wing proposed Jon Huntsman and Mitt Romney. The libertarian wing was ably represented by former Libertarian Party presidential nominee Ron Paul. Remaining were the four conservatives: Michele Bachman, Newt Gingrich, Rick Perry and Rick Santorum.

Of these candidates, Newt Gingrich had the best track record and the most detailed plan for the future. For all of his flaws, he was the candidate best equipped to debate Barack Obama.

The problem was that he was also an abomination to the party insiders, who always worked to overcome the grassroots majority and push their candidates through to the nomination. The big question was how the GOP would handle the tremendous party infighting still to come.

Republican Resolution: Reject Romney and RINOs

As the 2012 presidential election year started, conservatives faced a very old problem: how to wrest control of their party from the country club establishment which had dominated the process for generations.

While the grassroots of the Republican Party are solidly conservative, the power brokers are mostly moderates who could not care less about principle and are only concerned about power. For some it is financial gain through contracts and positions, for others it is access to the powerful in the federal government. In contrast, most conservatives are idealistic and do battle in the arena of ideas, while the establishment tries to hold on to their cushy relationships.

These influential insiders had long since picked their candidate for the 2012 presidential race: Multiple Choice Mitt Romney. While he might have been the right option for the special interest groups, he was not right for a majority of conservative Republicans. In Iowa, despite outspending his opponents, Romney lost the caucus. He even finished below his total from 2008.

This didn't concern the GOP power brokers, who believed Romney had the money and organization to win a lengthy and expensive race. He was their ideal candidate. He not only served as governor of the most liberal state in the nation, he was a millionaire with powerful connections all across the country.

Moreover, during the 2008 presidential election Romney had performed well and given John McCain plenty of competition. In 2012 he was more organized still, better funded, and had more experience. In the debates he performed flawlessly, giving well-rehearsed answers to softball questions. While his conservative opponents were savaged by the media and the GOP establishment, Romney soared above the fray, looking presidential.

But then there was a reason he did so well: for the prior six years he'd been working at only one job: running for president. He looked good and sounded smart, but the problem remained that he had no core convictions. During his career he had taken multiple stands on social, economic and foreign policy issues. When questioned, his answers were poll-tested and strictly political, not principled.

Disturbingly, although Romney was leading in the polls, he had never been called to account for his amazing contradictions on a host of issues, such as abortion, taxes, the influence of Ronald Reagan, climate change, gun control, and health care reform, to name just a few.

The beginning of 2012 was the perfect time for conservatives to take Romney to task and wrest the nomination away from the RINOs. Conservatives knew that Romney was sure to lose to Barack

Obama, which would subject the country to four more years of reckless liberalism. Only a united push from conservatives mounting a successful intraparty attack against Romney could prevent this outcome.

Although the media continually claimed that Romney was the only GOP candidate with a chance to appeal to moderates and Independents and beat Obama, recent political history indicated otherwise. Every time the Republican Party nominated a moderate like Romney, the party lost. In the past 35 years, these moderate Republican presidential nominees have all lost: Gerald Ford, George H. W. Bush, Bob Dole and John McCain. Only when the GOP nominated a conservative for president, Ronald Reagan, did party win. The one aberration was George W. Bush, a moderate who lost the popular vote in 2000, then won it in 2004, mostly due to Americans rallying around the flag after the attacks of 9/11. Bush also benefitted from a pathetic opponent in John Kerry and a huge evangelical turnout, as traditional marriage amendments were on the ballot across the country that year.

In 2012 the media spin was that a moderate GOP nominee would have a better chance of winning. In reality, a moderate candidate like Romney turned off not only conservatives, but also Libertarians and millions of disappointed Democrats who were looking for an alternative to Barack Obama. Romney offered nothing but a watered-down version of the real thing: Obama liberalism.

The Republican Party finally had a chance to give voters a choice, not an echo. The party needed to be represented by an optimistic, articulate conservative who could present a platform of "bold colors, not pale pastels." The GOP nominee needed to make it perfectly clear where he or she stood on the important issues facing this nation. With the economy in trouble, the borders unprotected and our country threatened by radicals plotting our destruction, we needed a strong conservative leader to step forward.

Clearly, Mitt Romney, the Massachusetts liberal, was not that leader. His gubernatorial record bore no resemblance to conservatism. By the end of his term, he had raised taxes by $730 million. It is little wonder that he called the flat tax proposal "unfair." He criticized Ronald Reagan while running for office as an Independent. Later he claimed he was really a "moderate" . . . with "progressive" ideas. While he was a good fit for Massachusetts, Romney was a horrible fit for the Republican Party.

Eventually, Romney boasted about a supposed "conversion" to more conservative positions like opposing abortion, but that looked to be done strictly for political convenience. In the 2012 race, Romney was clearly trying to fool uninformed voters who were easily manipulated by the media.

Nevertheless Romney received major assistance from the establishment wing of the Republican Party, and his fundraising far exceeded that of his opponents. They made a blatant attempt to buy the election. In Iowa, a Political Action Committee linked to Romney spent millions of dollars trying to destroy Newt Gingrich. The Speaker was hurt, but Romney was not particularly helped in the process.

Despite superior fundraising, organization and experience, Romney remained stuck at the 25 percent support level. Clearly the vast majority of Republican voters wanted a more conservative candidate. The Governor led only because moderates had united behind his candidacy, while the larger number of conservatives had split their hopes amongst six candidates. To win, conservatives needed to quickly unite behind a single candidate.

For Republicans, the best New Year's resolution in 2012 would have been to reject Romney and the RINO wing of the party. Conservatives knew that if a miracle occurred and Romney was elected president, he would not offer the type of change the country desperately needed. He would merely tinker with our colossal system of government.

The time for tinkering was over. With a rising national debt and 46 million Americans on food stamps, it was time for a massive course correction. The stakes were high and the presidential election was only months away. The Republican Party could not afford to nominate another moderate loser.

Sadly, the Party power brokers did not seem to grasp this reality.

The Rush to Coronate Romney

After just one caucus and one primary, a stampede of media analysts and Republican operatives rushed to proclaim Mitt Romney the *de facto* Republican nominee. Despite the fact that only a fraction of the delegates had been chosen and voters in 48 states had yet to cast a single vote, there was a definite push to call this political ballgame early.

Why the rush to coronate a nominee? After all, a prolonged primary battle would not harm Romney or whoever won the nomination; it would only make the GOP nominee stronger. Barack Obama had certainly became a better candidate during his hard-fought Democratic Party campaign against Hillary Clinton in 2008.

In contrast, Republicans had not seen a vigorous nomination contest since the epic 1976 race between Gerald Ford and Ronald Reagan. Unfortunately, the GOP usually favors establishment candidates who had previously lost and are running for the second or third time. Republicans like to clear the field for the candidate that insiders believe earned a spot at the top of the ticket. This flawed strategy gave the party two nominees who were major losers: Bob Dole and John McCain.

The 2012 race had an early front runner, Mitt Romney, who had lost in 2008 and never stopped running for president. With a massive war chest and a plethora of party leaders pushing for his nomination, the Massachusetts flip-flopper had plenty of momentum. Media analysts and commentators were ready to coronate Romney and declare that the race was over and the country would be subjected to a Romney versus Obama race in the fall.

After just Iowa and New Hampshire, it was too early to call the contest. Voters in the South think differently on most issues, and are clearly more conservative. Usually, a moderate candidate like Romney would lose in South Carolina. In this race, Romney benefitted from the media touting him as the eventual winner, along with a huge Super PAC fundraising advantage. While voters in South Carolina like to side with a winner and not "waste" their vote, they also don't want to vote for a moderate when there are conservative alternatives.

As the candidates entered South Carolina, moderates were united behind Romney and conservatives were split among the other candidates: Gingrich, Santorum and Perry. Unfortunately, the Tea Party did not have a unified voice; there was division among the right-leaning candidates. The longer this rift remained, the better the result for Romney.

In the Republican Party, it is always positive for conservatives to engage liberals, but only if it is a fair fight. In 2012, all of the establishment was united behind Romney, but the conservatives were split. For conservatives to improve their chances of defeating Romney, they needed to quickly unite behind a single candidate. But there was no consolidation. Instead, the conservative infighting continued and Romney continued on the path to the nomination.

Meanwhile, Democrats were praying that Romney would be the GOP nominee. They knew he was the weakest candidate they could face in the general election, regardless of the media spin. In fact, Democratic operative Donna Brazile admitted this on ABC after their network's Republican debate.

She knew that if Romney became the nominee, Republicans would not be able to challenge Obama on the issue of socialized medicine. After all, Romney's own Massachusetts plan had been the inspiration for the Obama healthcare disaster, and two of Romney's advisers helped Obama craft his plan.

Under Romney, taxes increased by $730 million in Massachusetts, so he would also not be able to make the anti-tax argument. While Romney was Governor, Massachusetts suffered from anemic economic growth, the fourth lowest in the country. Romney supported liberal judges and cabinet appointments. He espoused liberal positions on major issues and was a self-proclaimed "progressive" who did not want to "return to Reagan Bush." These liberal positions, the flip-flopping, and the controversy over his tenure at Bain Capital made Romney an inviting target for Obama and the Democrats.

The Republican electorate heard Romney sound conservative themes, but his record was spotty and his conversion had been made for convenience, not principle.

The problem with the nomination process was that Romney had not been completely vetted and most Republicans were unable to express their opinions. The nomination was dominated by states such as Iowa and New Hampshire that did not represent the main-stream of the Republican Party. The result? The process was shortcut by media pressure and big money, and the vast majority of GOP voters across this country were disenfranchised.

One year before the early primaries, the Tea Party had celebrated a major victory in the mid-term elections. But incredibly, by 2012 Mitt Romney was getting ready for his coronation, even though he did not represent the Tea Party or the conservative Reagan wing of the Republican Party.

To win, the conservative candidates had only one chance: they needed to set aside their personal interests and unite behind one candidacy. This would have required several candidates to end their campaigns, sacrificing personal ambitions for a greater cause: the advancement of conservatism. By consolidating on the conservative side they would give Romney and the establishment wing a run for their money. Instead, the union never occurred and the drumbeat that the competition was "over" continued. As a result, the Romney nomination was a conservative nightmare that eventually became a reality.

Liberal Media Misfires in Newt Attack

In the days before the South Carolina primary, the liberal media was up to its usual tricks. ABC News aired a heavily-promoted interview with one of Newt Gingrich's ex-wives in which she claimed that Gingrich had wanted an "open marriage." This was a predictable attack from an embittered ex-spouse; there was nothing new in the charge because the former Mrs. Gingrich had made similar claims in a previous magazine interview. What *was* new was the network's outrageous and deliberate attempt to manipulate election results by releasing the interview two days before the South Carolina Republican primary.

According to news reports, some ABC News executives wanted to postpone the air date of the interview until after the South Carolina vote. Predictably, the ethical voices within the network were dismissed by those who wanted to make a crass attempt to cash in on a ratings bonanza.

Gingrich was clearly offended by the story. When asked

about the issue during a CNN debate, he fired back at moderator John King, saying that he was "appalled that you would begin a presidential debate on a topic like that." The debate audience responded with a standing ovation, giving Gingrich a huge boost of support. It also showed that the media's "gotcha" tactics had backfired. Instead of derailing Gingrich, the story actually boosted his candidacy.

As Sarah Palin noted, conservatives were "sick of the politics of personal destruction, because it's played so selectively by the media, that their target, in this case Newt, he's now going to soar even more. Because we know the game now, and we just won't put up with it. Good call, media."

From the beginning of the 2012 race, the liberal media had been targeting the conservative GOP candidates. Vicious attacks were launched against Michele Bachmann and Herman Cain, forcing both of them to drop from the race. While conservatives endured blistering attacks and probes into their personal lives, President Obama was given the royal treatment, barely subjected to any tough questions.

Eight years after Barack Obama burst onto the national stage, the media had still not demanded a host of his records and personal information. Not surprisingly, much of Obama's background was still unknown. Instead of media outrage, there was silence, proving definitively that there was media bias and a huge double standard.

Although the liberal media attack on Gingrich and attempt to manipulate the vote failed miserably, Gingrich was never an acceptable nominee to the people who run the Republican Party— the people who were determined to award the nomination, come hell or high water, to Mitt Romney.

The Empire Strikes Back

After being pummeled by Newt Gingrich in a series of forums, Mitt Romney employed a new strategy in the January 23, 2012 debate in Tampa, Florida: he hired Brett O'Donnell as his debate coach. O'Donnell had previously worked with the Michele Bachmann campaign. According to Gingrich, O'Donnell's "specialty is to say as many untruths as fast as you can." In the debate Romney attacked Gingrich on everything from his tenure as Speaker of the House to his contract with Freddie Mac. In contrast, Gingrich was more subdued, and spent the evening responding to Romney's assault.

Although Romney's new tactics had an effect, what really harmed Gingrich was the dull debate crowd. In previous debates, Gingrich had thrived on connecting with conservative audiences, who rewarded him with several standing ovations. However, in Tampa, NBC Evening News Anchor Brian Williams asked the crowd to remain quiet. As a result, there were no standing ovations, no emotion and no energy. It was the perfect setting for the GOP establishment, the "empire," to strike back.

Since the massive Gingrich victory in the South Carolina primary, the GOP establishment had been in a total meltdown. The Republican insiders, lobbyists and consultants who thrive on politics-as-usual had been expecting Romney to breeze through the GOP race with little or no real competition. Gingrich's win in South Carolina alarmed the establishment. They began attacking him from the moment the South Carolina results were tabulated. On Fox News, personalities like Brit Hume and Ann Coulter, who is a true conservative on most issues, continued their efforts to dismiss and mock Gingrich. Romney deployed his surrogates to bash Gingrich on national television programs. New Jersey Governor Chris Christie claimed that Gingrich was "an embarrassment" to the Republican

Party. It was the same message that Romney was delivering in his television appearances. These attacks were buttressed by millions of dollars in Romney attack commercials airing throughout Florida.

Romney's Florida strategy was very similar to the one that had worked so well for him in Iowa. Gingrich had been leading in the polls for several weeks before the Iowa caucus, until Romney Super-PAC unleashed a multi-million-dollar media assault that effectively destroyed the Speaker. In Florida the Romney forces were hoping to work their negative media magic once again.

Moreover, Romney was not alone in trying to stop Gingrich; he had the support of almost all the Republican Party leaders. They were terrified of Gingrich because of his intelligence and his vow to use conservative policies to make a real change as president. The insiders never want real change; they want politics as usual.

The establishment always preferred Romney, who is a moderate in the mold of Gerald Ford and Bob Dole. He was a friend to the Beltway insiders who thrive on a growing bureaucracy. The insiders bet heavily on Romney and laid it all on the line to insure his nomination. They simply could not afford to nominate Gingrich; he was too unpredictable and radical.

Sadly, the power brokers ignored the Tea Party volunteers and conservative activists who work in the trenches and give small donations to the Republican Party. The insiders never cared about the Tea Party movement or the conservative agenda. In fact, their goal was to quash the true conservative wing of the party.

In South Carolina, Gingrich tapped into the Republican grassroots' growing resentment against both the liberal media and the GOP establishment. He used his emotion and passion for the country, as well as an ability to connect with people who feel ignored and discounted, to fuel his rise in the polls.

Of course, Romney never expressed anger toward the media or establishment, because both groups had always treated him well. The establishment wanted Romney nominated because he would safe-guard their jobs, while the mainstream media wanted him because they knew he would lose to their favorite candidate, Barack Obama.

The majority of Republicans had always wanted something different. For evidence, just look at the mid-term elections of 2010 and the avalanche of Tea Party conservatives who were elected across the country. These voters had not disappeared; they were just being ignored again. They wanted a conservative nominee who would aggressively take the race to President Obama. They did not believe the media narrative that a conservative would lose and that the GOP must move to the ideological center. The main problem with the Republican Party was that it had been stuck in the ideological center ever since Newt Gingrich left as House Speaker.

Despite the best efforts of the Tea Party members who had been elected to Congress in 2010, nothing had stopped the accumulation of trillions of dollars in federal debt and the ever-expanding reach of the federal government. The election of 2012 was a chance to complete the mission the Tea Party started in the previous election: beat President Obama and restore fiscal sanity to the country. It was also a chance to restore relevance to the Republican Party.

David Versus Goliath in 2012 Presidential Race

The last few weeks of January 2012 were a bruising time in the GOP race for president. The politics of personal destruction was alive and well in Florida, thanks to the attack machine of Mitt Romney, which spent $17 million destroying Newt Gingrich. Although the Speaker responded with his own attacks, he was overwhelmed by his better-funded opponent.

Although nasty, the race was certainly not unique. The stark contrast between a well-funded frontrunner and a conservative challenger was reminiscent of the 1976 GOP primary battle between incumbent president Gerald Ford and conservative challenger Ronald Reagan. Ford was the heavy favorite and enjoyed all of the establishment support. He was well-funded and considered the presumptive nominee; however, Reagan had other ideas. The California conservative battled Ford all the way to the convention before losing in a razor-thin contest that set the stage for his ultimate nomination in 1980.

Both times that Reagan ran for president, the GOP establishment arrayed itself against him. Newt Gingrich faced a similar problem in 2012. He lost Florida because of the onslaught of attacks and two poor debate performances. His momentum from South Carolina became a distant memory in the ever-changing presidential race. Now his goal was to hang on until Super Tuesday on March 6, and hopefully capture enough delegates to give his campaign a boost for the long months ahead.

But Romney has the ultimate advantage: money. He was supported by the big money donors of the GOP, as well as personally being a multi-millionaire who could dump almost unlimited funds into the race. Although Gingrich's Super-PAC was funded by a Nevada millionaire, his campaign depended on support from the small donors and grassroots Republicans who populate Tea Party organizations across the country.

To no one's surprise, Gingrich won the straw poll of the Florida Tea Party Patriots. Most Tea Party members never trusted Romney because of his well-documented liberal record in Massachusetts. There was also disgust at the scorched-earth campaign he had employed against Gingrich and his other opponents. Sarah Palin called it the "tactics of the left." She was right—and if anyone was an expert on receiving personal attacks, it was Sarah Palin.

Among their many assaults, Romney and his allies claimed that Gingrich was anti-Reagan, even though Newt had been one of the Congressmen working the hardest for the conservative agenda throughout his career. In fact, Newt had received the endorsement of someone who was an expert on the Reagan legacy: the president's son, Michael. At a 1995 dinner, Nancy Reagan said that "Barry Goldwater handed the torch to Ronnie, and in turn Ronnie turned that torch over to Newt and the Republican members of Congress to keep that dream alive." Newt was the rightful conservative heir to Reagan, while Romney was nothing but a political opportunist.

Back when Newt was fighting liberals in Congress, Romney was a registered Independent voting for liberal presidential candidates like Jimmy Carter in 1980 and Paul Tsongas in 1992. In a 1994 debate, Romney claimed that he "did not want to go back to Reagan-Bush" policies. Clearly, Romney's Republican pedigree was weak, yet the media kept anointing him as smart choice for the GOP.

The moderate insiders hated the grassroots conservatives of the Tea Party who demanded smaller government and a return to the U.S. Constitution. The insiders wanted government to grow, only with Republicans getting the contracts. The Tea Party actually wanted to end the politics-as-usual system that the Democratic and Republican establishments both cherished. This is why the movement was such a threat and why Gingrich, the Tea Party's favorite presidential candidate, was targeted for destruction.

After Florida, there were calls from Republican insiders and the media to unite behind Romney and for the other candidates to end their campaigns. This was being proposed even though there were still voters in 46 states who had not had a chance to cast a ballot.

The establishment knew the stakes: if they won the nomination, they would wrest control of the party back from the Tea Party. On the other hand, if Gingrich won the nomination, the Tea Party faithful would be energized and the grassroots would have won a historic battle against the establishment for only the second time in modern history.

As usual, the GOP presidential race was a true David vs. Goliath story—and as history notes, the underdog wins every now and then. Despite the Florida results, the Republican underdog still had a slight chance. Although the fat lady was warming up, she had not yet begun to sing.

Santorum Speaks for Spiritual Majority

By late February 2012, the GOP presidential race had undergone dramatic changes. Because Gingrich's chances had been badly damaged, the most serious challenger to Mitt Romney had become Rick Santorum. The former Pennsylvania Senator was leading in the national polls, and even competing with Romney in Romney's home state of Michigan.

Why did Santorum surge to the front? While he was a strong conservative on fiscal issues and supported tax cuts to spur economic growth, he was largely known as a "culture warrior." He focused most of his attention on social issues and was able to tap into a very deep reservoir of discontent that millions of Americans had with our country's culture, educational institutions, media, and political officials.

Average, hard-working Americans sensed there was something deeply wrong with a country that highlighted celebrities who mock the Catholic Church at the Grammy Awards or give the middle finger salute to the American people at the Super Bowl.

In the past few decades, Americans have witnessed the music industry, television, movies and our universities celebrate radical liberalism and attack the Judeo-Christian foundations of the nation. There is an ongoing battle in our culture between good and evil, and people of faith had been looking for a candidate who would forcefully address this problem. The faith-based voters of America finally found their voice in the candidacy of Rick Santorum.

In a 2008 speech to Ave Maria University in Florida, Santorum painted a deeply disturbing picture of America. He said that Satan, "the father of lies," had set his sights on this country. According to Santorum, "Satan is attacking the great institutions of America, using those great vices of pride, vanity, and sensuality as the root to attack all of the strong plants that has so deeply rooted in the American tradition."

When this speech was posted by the Drudge Report, the mainstream media went into a tizzy, denouncing Santorum as a religious extremist. But instead of being extreme, Santorum was accurately painting a picture of America today. He simply noted that Satan is attacking the universities, culture, Christian church and political environment in America.

Few can deny the "spiritual war" being waged in our nation. Santorum warned Americans about the dangers of turning away from our faith-based roots and following beliefs that are not centered on God.

Along with accurately describing our country, Santorum alerted Americans to the dangers of the Obama agenda. In a speech to a Tea Party group in Ohio, Santorum said that the president follows "some phony ideal, some phony theology. Oh, not a theology based on the Bible—a different theology." He was not claiming that Obama was a Muslim, but that he adhered to radical liberal beliefs, such as environmental extremism. Santorum defined this type of theology as the "idea that man is here to serve the Earth, as opposed to husband its resources and being good stewards of the Earth."

In his view, this was "a phony ideal" and dangerous to our

country. For many New Age leftists, radical environmentalism had become a new religion. Instead of worshipping God, they worshipped the earth. They mistook the creation for the Creator. Unlike the rest of the candidates in the race, Santorum had the guts to address these sensitive issues directly.

By the Spring of 2012 it had become apparent that the election might well be decided on these issues rather than the economy, which is often the deciding factor. Even though most Americans didn't think their own financial situation seemed particularly good, according to media reports, the economy was improving. Obama could be counted on to tout such reports in his quest for re-election.

Rick Santorum bet that the 2012 election would be decided on different issues. While there was debate about the actual status of the American economy, there was little question about our culture and the state of the basic institutions in our country. Millions of Americans saw what was happening in their schools and in the media, and wanted change. The vast majority of these voters, the backbone of the Republican Party, were social conservatives looking for a candidate like Santorum. They wanted someone who would voice their concerns that if America did not have a course correction, it was headed for ruin.

Back in the 1992 presidential race, GOP candidate Pat Buchanan had discussed a raging "cultural war" in our country. Few would argue that the culture had deteriorated significantly since that time. In 2012 Santorum hoped to win the nomination and defeat Obama in the general election by focusing on the cultural issues that the mainstream media contended were not important.

Fortunately, the mainstream media never did represent the vast majority of Americans. While the economy is always a very important matter, Santorum hoped to convince the Republican electorate that the party could not win by focusing only on the nation's finances. He implored that it was time for a cultural course correction; time to stop the moral decline.

Millions of Americans agreed. They were looking for a candidate who understood their concerns and could articulate them, despite an avalanche of ridicule from the mainstream media. These spiritual voters found their presidential candidate in Rick Santorum, who boldly proclaimed his faith and did not apologize for being a Christian.

The question remained if there were enough social conservative voters to prevail against Mitt Romney in the Republican primaries. While many people wanted a spiritual awakening in the nation, as the GOP race continued it seemed unlikely that these voters constituted a majority.

Nominating Romney was a Sketchy Strategy for the GOP

"Well, I think you hit a reset button for the fall campaign.... Everything changes, it's almost like an Etch-A-Sketch. You can kind of shake it up and we start all over again." —Eric Fehrnstrom, Romney Campaign Communications Adviser. CNN interview, Wednesday, March 21, 2012

In the wake of Fehrnstrom's gaffe, the stock price of Etch-A-Sketch soared. Newt Gingrich and Rick Santorum brought the classic children's toy with them on campaign stops throughout Louisiana. Once again, Romney had to address concerns that he was a flip-flopper who, if he won the Republican nomination, would once again revert to moderate positions in the general election.

The slip overshadowed good news for Romney. By winning the Illinois primary on March 20, he had claimed approximately half the delegates he needed to win the Republican nomination. He also received an endorsement from former Florida Governor Jeb Bush and a virtual endorsement from U.S. Senator Jim DeMint (R-SC), who all but recommended that Rick Santorum and Newt Gingrich withdraw from the race.

The Republican establishment also rallied more than ever behind Romney. The insiders and power brokers wanted the nomination contest to end so that the party could focus on beating President Obama in November. The party bosses saw the contested primaries as a negative force that prevented the electorate from uniting behind Romney.

This position was certainly not accepted by those voters who supported the conservative candidates. In addition, a quick closure to the nomination battle would, in effect, disenfranchise GOP voters in the states holding contests later in the election cycle. A prolonged contest would allow voters in all states, not just early states like Iowa and New Hampshire, to participate in nominating a candidate.

Also, despite Romney's victories, conservative voters continued to be distrustful of him—and for good reason. They wanted a candidate who stood firm on principle and would not be swayed by the liberal media or the institutional forces of political correctness.

What they saw in Romney was the direct opposite of this ideal. Over the years he had changed his position on practically every issue. He was campaigning as a conservative and insisted he loved Ronald Reagan, even though he had called himself a "progressive" when running for office in Massachusetts.

Upon completing his term as Governor, Romney left Massachusetts with a big deficit thanks to having raised taxes to support liberal policies such as abortion, cap and trade, and socialized medicine.

This provided a huge advantage to Democrats. Obama knew that if he were to be matched against Romney in the presidential race, all he would have to do was revisit Romney's previous record and expose his obscene policy changes. Obama was also prepared to tell voters that his own healthcare program was modeled on Romney's. He could say that he agreed with the Massachusetts version of Romney—the one who believed in abortion, gay marriage and global warming.

It was amazing. Sixteen months after the Tea Party had ushered into power a Republican Congress, the presidential candidate with the fewest ties to that group was being pushed toward the nomination by Republican Party leaders.

In the interview quoted above, Fehrnstrom was merely being candid about his boss. Governor Romney had a history of saying and doing *anything* to be elected. There was no reason to believe he would not do the same thing as the nominee or as president. What *was* certain was that he would not pursue a conservative agenda. Nominating him would be a sketchy strategy for a party that supposedly wanted to win the White House.

Mitt's Conservative Masquerade Ends

Once Romney secured the GOP nomination, he was free to be himself—and as expected, his masquerade as a conservative ended. He returned to many of the moderate-to-liberal stances he had held as Governor of the People's Republic of Massachusetts, and once again became a polite politician who treated his Democratic opponents with respect.

Mitt Romney turned nasty only against other Republicans. In the GOP primary, the Governor had eviscerated his opponents with high-priced, non-stop, hard-hitting attacks. But he did not employ the same tactics in his general election showdown against President Obama, whom he continued to refer to as a "nice guy."

While Romney was playing nice, Barack Obama was going on a rampage, tearing the U.S. Constitution to shreds. On June 15, 2012, in the White House Rose Garden, Obama decided to issue *de facto* amnesty to 1.4 million aliens who had illegally entered the country at a young age. The president evidently decided that standing immigration laws did not apply to this category of individuals, who were thus able to apply for work permits and no longer faced the threat of deportation. To the 23 million unemployed Americans looking for work, this was a slap in the face—they would have to face more competition for scarce jobs.

Romney's response to this outrageous move was to seek "common ground" on the immigration issue. During an interview on *Face the Nation* he refused, on five occasions, to say whether as president he would rescind the Obama policy.

A few days later, Obama issued a questionable Executive Privilege order protecting his Attorney General from Congressional investigators and covering up documents that dealt with the scandalous Fast and Furious program, which had resulted in the death of a Border Patrol agent. In response, Romney should have condemned the president's order, demanding that Attorney General Holder resign and insisting on full transparency and the release of all documents. Instead, Romney's response was nonexistent. He was even "largely silent" on the Fast and Furious debacle.

On June 24, 2012, the Supreme Court struck down three of the major provisions of the state of Arizona's law dealing with illegal immigration. The justices upheld the remaining provision, which allowed law enforcement to question suspected illegal aliens about their immigration status. After the ruling, it took the Obama Department of Homeland Security only a few hours to rescind agreements with seven law enforcement agencies in Arizona. Thus, the federal government would no longer provide assistance to Arizona in dealing with illegal immigrant arrests, unless the illegal had a felony in his or her criminal history. Horace Cooper of the National Center for Public Policy characterized the administration's move "a complete disregard of the Constitutional process." Arizona Governor Jan Brewer was more succinct: he said that Obama had told Arizona to "drop dead."

With a Republican Governor and the U.S. Constitution under attack from the White House, what did presumptive GOP nominee Mitt Romney say? His spokesman refused to condemn the Supreme Court ruling or to offer support for the Arizona immigration law. In fact, after being hounded by reporters for an answer and evading 20 questions on the issue, Romney spokesman Rick Gorka offered this meek response: "The Governor supports the right of states; that's all we're going to say on the issue."

When the people of Arizona, the conservative movement and the GOP needed a champion, Romney hid under his moderate cloak—yet another indication that the worries of conservatives about Romney were well-founded. If he had been elected president, he would have been like Bush 41 and Bush 43, managing the growth of government rather than seriously curtailing it. He would have worked *with* Democrats instead of opposing their socialist agenda. He would have used government to "solve" problems rather than providing the only real solution: limited government.

During the 2012 general election, so-called political experts had pushed Romney to move toward the middle. They said in order to win, he had to reject conservatism, even though millions of

Americans were thirsting for a conservative alternative to Obama. These voters wanted a real choice, not an echo.

Romney should have been clearly differentiating his positions with the president on *all* issues, not just the economy. For example, he should have realized that illegal immigration was a vitally important issue. Voters along the southern border with Mexico felt overrun by illegal immigrants, and they were frustrated by a federal government which refused to take action.

Instead, Romney tried to placate the Latino vote by toning down his rhetoric on this issue. During the Republican primaries he had expressed staunch support for the Arizona immigration law—but in the general election, his spokesman went to great lengths to avoid discussing the issue at all.

Sadly, this was just more evidence that Romney did not possess the conservative principles that the Republican Party and this nation desperately needed. It proved once again why his candidacy doomed the Republican Party to defeat in the general election.

The nation will soon have a president to succeed Obama—but that person will never be Mitt Romney, not matter how many times he entertains presidential ambitions.

Earth to Romney: Obamacare is a Tax

Throughout the presidential race, the misguided and ill-equipped Romney campaign kept making mistakes. Mere days after the presumptive GOP nominee refused to comment on the Fast and Furious investigation, criticize the president's executive order of *de facto* amnesty for 1.4 million illegal aliens, or comment on the Supreme Court decision striking down the Arizona immigration law, the Romney campaign once again showed its weakness.

In an interview on MSNBC, Romney advisor Eric Fehrnstrom declared the Affordable Healthcare Act (Obamacare) to be a "penalty" rather than a tax. This idiotic declaration was made even though Republican leaders had spent the previous four days denouncing the legislation as a tax by using the convoluted reasoning of Chief Justice John Roberts. The Supreme Court called it a tax, so it was a tax, whether the Romney campaign agreed with this horrible judicial ruling or not.

Fehrnstrom had just undercut the best line of attack Republicans had against this massive takeover of the healthcare industry. Why did he make such a foolish mistake? Apparently the Romney campaign was worried that Democrats would call his Massachusetts healthcare plan a tax as well. Of course it *was* a tax, as well as a mini-version of Obamacare. It was a state government takeover of a healthcare system. From all reports, it failed miserably, as Obamacare was destined to do on a national basis.

What made Obamacare worse than Romney's plan was that it was much larger, and had been jammed through Congress without the support of the American people or the medical industry. Thanks to the Supreme Court's ruling, Obamacare was characterized as a massive tax increase, even though it was never represented in that manner during the Congressional debate. The end result was that the legislation represented the largest middle class tax increase in our nation's history.

If Republicans had portrayed the legislation as what it really was—a tax increase—they could have convinced Americans to oppose both the legislation and its chief proponent, President Barack Obama. Despite the spin from the media and the administration, the American economy was weak and, in a lousy economy almost everyone opposes a tax increase.

The issue was tailor-made for the Romney campaign; they should have run with it all the way to victory. Unfortunately, Mitt the Massachusetts Moderate did not get the message. Through his spokesman, Fehrnstrom, he made it clear he intended to tone down the rhetoric once again. This was exactly the wrong approach to take to beat Obama. It was the same flawed strategy used by John McCain in 2008, and Republicans should have remembered what happened to him.

In order to win, Romney needed to go the opposite direction and employ the same brass-knuckle strategy he'd used against his GOP opponents in the primary. He'd shown no mercy toward Next Gingrich and Rick Santorum, so why did he go soft on President Obama? Because he was listening to Fehrnstrom and the other Massachusetts liberals who advised him. As Rupert Murdoch noted on his Twitter account, Romney needed to "drop...old friends from team and hire...some real pros." He predicted that without an overhaul of advisers, Romney's chances were "doubtful."

As Joel Pollak stated on Breitbart.com, "conservatives...exhort: Mitt, start fighting, or give up and let someone else do it.... No one wants to watch another conservative capitulate to Obama." The problem for Republicans was that the party's last several presidential nominees had not been true conservatives. They had cared more about Beltway pundits than following commonsense conservative principles.

The liberal media and moderate Republican political establishment did not want to see the Republican nominee vigorously attack Obama on hot-button issues. McCain had listened to these "sensible" voices that told him to play fair with Obama. Romney never realized that this strategy was completely flawed.

Meanwhile the Tea Party members and the conservative base of the Republican Party waited in vain for Romney to follow the advice of Ronald Reagan and run a campaign based on "no pale pastels, but bold colors, which make it unmistakably clear" where he stood on the issues.

Sadly, Romney failed to follow the tried and true Reagan formula.

Romney Unplugged Better than Romney on the Stump

On the campaign trail and in media interviews, Mitt Romney was always very cautious, making bland comments on the issues of the day. Only in "off the record" chats with major donors did he tell the real, unvarnished truth. This led to a serious media scandal in mid-September. It was such a major story that Romney appeared at a hastily-arranged news conference to respond to the leaked video taken at a fundraising dinner on May 17 in Boca Raton, Florida.

In the video, Romney said that "There are 47 percent of the people who will vote for the president no matter what…. There are 47 percent who are with him, who are dependent on government, who believe that, that they are victims, who believe that government has the responsibility to care for them, who believe that they are entitled to health care, to food, to housing."

In this supposedly private speech, Romney also stated that "my job is not to worry about those people…I'll never convince them they should take personal responsibility and care for their lives…. What I have to do is convince the five percent to ten percent in the center that are independents, that are thoughtful."

In other words, all Romney did was tell a small group of supporters some basic facts about the electorate: to win, he needed to appeal to undecided Independent voters rather than those who were not paying taxes, all of whom were most likely in Obama's camp. This comment was twisted by the media into a statement that Romney did not care about 47% of the electorate. In reality, he was merely admitting that he could not focus on that group of voters and needed to concentrate on those he *could* attract.

In the event, Romney was basically telling the truth: Obama had created a huge percentage of Americans who paid no income taxes yet received government services. Most, but not all, of these voters supported the president, while the majority of taxpaying citizens supported Romney. In the 2012 election, both candidates, like so many others, appealed to the small number of Independents who resided, as usual, "in the middle."

As a Massachusetts moderate with a very mixed voting record, Romney should have been concerned about keeping the GOP base happy and making sure those voters turned out in huge numbers on Election Day. Sadly, he was having a hard time closing the deal. For example, in an interview on *Meet the Press* he said he would retain parts of the president's healthcare plan, an idea that was anathema to conservatives who had used the healthcare bill to motivate millions of voters in the 2010 mid-term election.

In his comments, Romney was obviously trying to win the support of his liberal interrogator, but he should have realized that as the Republican nominee, he would be opposed by the media no matter what he said. As evidence, all he had to do was look at what happened to the media's favorite Republican, John McCain, in the 2008 presidential campaign. Once Obama became the nominee in 2008, the media abandoned McCain in droves and threw him to the wolves.

To win a victory, Romney needed to keep conservatives happy. He needed a united party, for he was facing an incumbent president running with a united Democratic Party supported by labor unions, Hollywood, special interest groups and the liberal news media.

By mid-September, the race had grown tight. A Gallup poll had Obama with a slim 47-46% lead: basically a dead heat. The president was especially vulnerable on three issues: the economy, high energy/gas prices, and national security.

It was clear that the economy was weak and gas prices were high, but the national security issue came into play as a surprise. The anti-American uprising in the Middle East had certainly not been expected, for the president had declared that our major terrorist foe was "on the run."

This situation gave Romney the perfect opportunity to make the case that the president's policies were weak and ineffective. Even with Obama showing support and empathy for the Muslim world, there had been violent protests, the storming of our embassies and the burning of the American Flag in over a dozen countries. The most serious tragedy involved the appalling deaths of four Americans in Benghazi, Libya, including our Ambassador Christopher Stevens. It was the first time in 33 years that a U.S. Ambassador had been murdered on foreign soil. Clearly, the whole tragedy would have been avoided if proper security had been in place and if the administration had listened to the Libyan government that warned of a 9/11-inspired attack.

Almost immediately after the incident, the Obama administration started spinning a lie; that the attack was caused by a crude 14-minute video entitled the "Innocence of Muslims," produced by an obscure California filmmaker who was later imprisoned. In reality, the video had nothing to do with the attack, the position was preposterous, and conflicted with the statements of numerous Libyan officials.

During the campaign Romney had many opportunities to talk directly to the American people. He should have questioned Obama about the lack of security for the ambassador and why the administration had not listened to warnings about an attack.

He had a great opportunity to be direct and forceful, as he had been in the leaked fundraising dinner video. If he had simply told the truth to the American people about the economy, energy and national security, and he would have won the election. Instead, he listened to advisers who insisted that the American people could not handle the truth. He chose the losing path.

Take Off Your Mitts, Governor Romney

With five weeks left until Election Day, the presidential race was very close. The mainstream media declared President Obama ahead, but Fox News analysts Dick Morris and Karl Rove showed Romney ahead.

Whatever the exact poll numbers, clearly the race was tight. Yet, given the situation in the country and throughout the world, the election should have been a landslide for the Republican nominee. The economy was horrible, the Middle East was in flames, our culture was in shambles and race relations had deteriorated since Obama took office. By almost every test, the president had failed miserably. He had not fulfilled his promises, such as cutting the deficit in half, creating more jobs, bringing a greater measure of peace to the Arab World or helping to heal a divided nation. Instead, Barack Obama was the most divisive president in history.

The liberal news media never did tell this true story completely or fairly, so it rested on the Republican presidential candidate to set the record straight. On this measure, Governor Romney was a total failure. Sadly, he was a very poor communicator.

By the fall, the candidate who had eviscerated his Republican opponents in the primaries was long gone. Voters witnessed Romney playing the role of the "gentleman" in his matchup against Obama. To win, he needed to take off the mitts and aggressively challenge Obama on his record all across the board. But Governor Romney wanted to focus strictly on the economy, while many other issues cried for attention and could have been used rally conservatives and Independents to his campaign.

Romney also allowed the media to sidetrack his message with a variety of bogus issues, including the "bombshell" video taken at the Florida fundraising dinner in May. He was also forced to play defense on issues such as his tax returns. To win, he should have played offense and made President Obama defend his woeful record. It was Obama who should have been on the defensive.

To woo the undecided, Romney needed to convince them they were *not* better off under Obama, and the country was *not* moving in the right direction. He needed to convince voters to "fire" Obama and hire someone else for the job.

Some voters saw Obama as a likeable, well-meaning person; Romney needed to dispel that notion. He should have educated voters about Obama's radical roots, radical mentors, radical philosophy and radical agenda. It was impossible for Romney to do this by being a gentleman and playing "nice." In politics, nice guys finish last. In 2008, John McCain played "nice" against Barack Obama and finished with 46% of the vote, losing in an Electoral College landslide. To avoid that scenario, Romney needed to be honest, straightforward and direct with the American people about the dangers of a second Obama term.

It was not just that Obama would wreck the economy even more. Romney should have outlined how as president he would handle radical Islam and counteract the spread of this dangerous ideology in the Middle East and Northern Africa. He should have been candid about Obama's divisive rhetoric, class warfare and racially-charged politics. The Governor should have provided voters with an alternative plan on how he would heal our country both culturally and economically.

He should have made the case that the stakes of the election were extremely high. He should have noted that voters faced a fork in the road. He should have asked, "Do we continue down the road to socialism, division and appeasement, or not?"

Mitt Romney needed to clearly explain to the American people why a second Obama term would be so dangerous. He needed to show emotion, outrage and courage, and take President Obama on directly. Doing so would have been uncomfortable for Governor Romney, but it was the only way he was going to win.

Just Say No
to Liberal Moderators

The election of 2012 featured another presidential campaign in which Americans were subjected to unfair and unbalanced debates. The moderators included Jim Lehrer of PBS, who exercised no control over the proceedings; liberal Martha Raddatz of ABC, who allowed Vice president Joe Biden to interrupt Congressman Paul Ryan 82 times; and Candy Crowley of CNN, who played the role of media blocking-back for President Obama. It was Crowley who shut down the Benghazi issue and confirmed that the president did call it a terror attack. In fact, her characterization was inaccurate and her involvement resulted in a major assist for Obama.

Both Mitt Romney and Paul Ryan did well in debate environments that were not necessarily fair. In the first debate, Romney had clearly won with an outstanding performance; however, Lehrer allowed President Obama four additional minutes of air time.

Raddatz did an even worse job by allowing Biden to mug for the camera and prevent viewers from hearing many of Ryan's answers. According to Chris Wallace of Fox News, Biden's performance was "unprecedented," as Ryan was especially mistreated. In fact, Wallace claimed that he had never "seen a debate in which one participant was an openly disrespectful of the other as Biden was to Paul Ryan... It was openly contemptuous."

Other commentators noted that Biden was "rude" and "cranky." This was Joe Biden being himself, an unpleasant sight to behold. The American public could have been spared this obnoxious behavior if the moderator had exercised some control over Biden. Instead, Ms. Raddatz gave the vice president free reign to hog the spotlight, and an extra 80 seconds to spew out his demagoguery. In contrast, she interrupted Paul Ryan 31 times and asked him much tougher questions.

In the debate, Raddatz was clearly doing the bidding of the Democrats. This meant that Ryan was debating not just Biden but also Raddatz. Although Ryan was good, facing two opponents made his task far more challenging. Raddatz was as biased as any debate moderator in history, but her performance should not have surprised anyone. It was eventually revealed that Barack Obama had been a guest at her first wedding. She would later attend the wedding of Michelle and Barack Obama with her ex-husband, who was subsequently appointed FCC Commissioner by President Obama.

These revelations were disturbing and indicated a personal connection between Raddatz and Obama. The relationship might not have ended in the early 1990s, for it was revealed that Raddatz visited the White House on December 18, 2009. Although the purpose of the visit was not disclosed, it did raise additional questions about the leanings of Raddatz. To make matters even worse, on March 26, 2012 Raddatz visited Vice president Biden at his residence as part of a ceremony marking Women's History Month.

Once all of these connections between Raddatz and the president and vice president were uncovered, she should have resigned as debate moderator. Not surprisingly, she refused to do so, and the Commission on Presidential Debates took no action. Any reputable group of impartial journalists would have issued an apology and selected another moderator. Sadly, the Commission has always leaned to the ideological left and was biased against Republicans.

The only conclusion to draw was that the Commission on Presidential Debates, which selected the moderators for all of the debates, was not impartial. In 2012, all four of the debate moderators were liberal, so the Commission failed to provide a fair and balanced forum for the American people.

Another presidential debate moderator was Bob Schieffer of CBS, a dyed-in-the-wool liberal "journalist" who regularly used his *Face the Nation* program to promote Democratic politicians and liberal policies. Republicans should have recognized the bias of the Commission since no reporter or anchor from Fox News had ever been chosen for the debates. Even though Fox News is more moderate than conservative, it stands out from the other more liberal networks. This uniqueness is the reason that Fox News enjoys much higher ratings than the other cable news outlets.

The Romney campaign and the Republican Party should not have participated in the debate under this kind of biased format. They should have rejected the liberal moderators and threatened to not participate unless more balanced selections were made. If Romney and Ryan had withdrawn, the Commission would have been forced to choose objective journalists.

Unfortunately, the arrangement in 2012 was no different from any other election year. In every debate, Republicans candidates allowed the Commission to stack the deck against them. This did a disservice to not only the election process, but, more importantly, to the American people.

The Republican Party:
The Political Insane Asylum

*"The definition of insanity is doing the same thing over and over
again and expecting different results."*
–Albert Einstein

Not surprisingly, between the horrific Romney campaign, the biased media and the uninspired electorate, the election proved to be another rout in favor of the Democratic Party. On Election Day, President Obama defeated Mitt Romney by almost five million popular votes and 126 electoral votes.

The president won every battleground state except one, and ushered into Congress an additional two Democrats in the Senate and eight in the House. While Obama recorded 3.5 million fewer votes than he had in 2008, Romney received only one million more votes than the pathetic total John McCain had reached. Overall, the two candidates did not inspire a very high turnout, as it declined from 61.6% in 2008 to 58.2% in 2012.

Although the election was not an Obama landslide, it was nowhere near the nail-biter many GOP pundits and consultants had predicted it would be. In fact, many of these supposed geniuses forecast a Romney "landslide." The so-called experts Dick Morris and Karl Rove both looked incredibly foolish in the aftermath.

In their post-election analysis, many of these same "experts" gave poisonous advice to a party already in serious trouble. They recommended the party move in the direction of Democrats on issues such as illegal immigration, gay marriage, drug use, taxes and abortion, to name a few. Following such advice would have been the death knell of the Republican Party.

Yet the party's moderate establishment had not only rejected the conservative agenda, it had made sure to control the party's nominee and the type of campaign he conducted. Every viable conservative candidate had been savaged by the party elite backing Romney's candidacy. They had been joined by the Fox News commentators, powerful pollsters like Karl Rove and Dick Morris, and influential columnists like George Will and Ann Coulter. All of them claimed the Romney was the most electable candidate—and, in the end, all of them were wrong.

After wasting a billion dollars on feckless advertising, Romney barely surpassed McCain's anemic level of support. Romney did not inspire or motivate the conservative GOP base, and, thus, lost a quarter of the evangelical vote on Election Day. These voters knew Romney was uncomfortable with social issues and had switched his position on everything from gay marriage to abortion.

In the general election, Romney did not employ the same tough and aggressive tactics against Barack Obama that he effectively used against his GOP opponents in the primary season. Like John McCain in 2008, Romney's kid glove treatment of the president was an utter failure. There was no better example than in the last debate, when Romney played nice with the president and agreed with many of his positions on foreign policy. Tragically, he refused to criticize the president for his deception and disastrous handling of the Benghazi terrorist attack.

Romney's campaign was the political equivalent of a football team playing the "prevent defense" trying not to lose rather than trying to win. This led the GOP nominee to disregard the "Fast and Furious" scandal and the president's decision to give amnesty to millions of illegal aliens under the age of 30. Worst of all, the president's unpopular plan to socialize healthcare was not attacked by the Romney campaign, thus wasting a powerful issue. As the father of socialized medicine in Massachusetts, Romney was the worst possible candidate to criticize "Obamacare," so he solved that problem by ignoring it altogether.

Romney ignored many good issues and spent almost his entire campaign focused on the issue of the economy, an important one, but not the only one. As a result, social conservatives were given no reason to vote. The grassroots movement that delivered the House of Representatives to the Republican Party, the Tea Party, was completely ignored by the Romney campaign. Tea Party favorites, like former Alaska Governor Sarah Palin, were not even invited to the party's convention in Tampa. To add insult to injury, Ron Paul's delegates were rudely treated in Tampa and many of them were denied credentials to the convention. The Romney team wanted a "unanimous" convention, but it was a counterproductive tactic as disgruntled Ron Paul supporters did not forget this disgraceful treatment.

Will the GOP ever learn? The correct tactic was not to become more like Democrats but to nominate a candidate with the courage to embrace the conservative principles outlined in the Republican platform. In contrast, Mitt Romney treated the platform like it was the bubonic plague.

Another Boehner Boondoggle

After the stunning loss in the 2012 presidential race, House Speaker John Boehner was unable to muster enough support for his "Plan B" proposal. The Congress adjourned for the holidays before supporting a plan that raised taxes on those making over $1 million per year, and offered only limited spending cuts over 10 years that would do nothing to solve our underlying fiscal problems.

By December of 2012, the nation's national debt stood at $16.3 trillion and the federal government had been running annual deficits of over $1 trillion for the previous five years. Clearly, the nation did not have a revenue problem—it had a major spending problem.

Both President Obama and Congress were incapable of cutting this monstrous federal budget. The fact that Boehner's "Plan B" proposal included limited spending cuts and increased tax rates was a major concession to President Obama. Although this plan was originally supported by Senate Democrats, it was rejected by President Obama, who demanded even more tax increases and fewer spending cuts.

The Boehner plan was also rejected by House conservatives who did not want any type of tax increase. House Republicans had been elected on a platform of low taxes, reduced government spending and limited government. Any type of support for "Plan B" or a similar tax increase would have betrayed the voters who elected the Republicans to office.

In contrast, President Obama had been elected the first time on a platform of bashing George W. Bush, and re-elected by demonizing Mitt Romney as a cruel rich guy. Obama had not been elected to raise taxes, as most Americans understand that increased taxes only lead to job losses. Increased taxes might force wealthy Americans who own businesses to reduce the size of their labor force, throwing more Americans out of work.

Sadly, Boehner and Obama refused to acknowledge that the best way to grow the economy and lower the unemployment rate was to offer a combination of serious tax cuts and major reductions in federal spending. Due to the spending habits of both Republicans and Democrats, in 2012 the federal government's expenditures consumed approximately 25% of the nation's GDP, whereas it had been only 18% in 2000, when the country last enjoyed a budget surplus.

Former House Speaker Newt Gingrich advised Republicans to reject a bogus solution like "Plan B." Instead he recommended that they hold hearings on out-of-control federal spending. It was a great idea because it would have educated Americans about the real problem: outrageous deficit spending. Of course, since it *was* a great idea, Boehner rejected it.

Ideally, Boehner should have been replaced as Speaker, for he continued to push for a tax increase. He should have led Congress to approve real, substantial tax cuts, including reform that eliminated unfair tax deductions and exemptions. The Republican Congress should have sent that bill to Senate and dared them to reject it.

Instead, the moderates led by Boehner continued to reject conservative ideas and refused to turn the tables on President Obama. The House GOP declined to stand firm on the principles outlined in their platform and continued to be railroaded by the media, liberals in Congress, and Barack Obama. This was not what the Tea Party had expected when they gave the GOP control of the House in 2010. In fact, it was the last thing they would have predicted would happen to their "revolution."

VI

2013

Is it Time for a Third Party?

By early January of 2013 it had become clear that the Republican Party had once again disappointed grassroots conservatives. That was when, with the help of GOP votes, Congress approved a catastrophic bill to avert a fall over the fiscal cliff.

The bill featured $41 in tax increases for every $1 in spending cuts. It added $4 trillion to the national debt. In a country that already faced a national debt of $16.423 trillion, it was an outrage that more substantial spending cuts and entitlement reform were not included in the legislation.

In the midst of a horrible economy, the bill increased income taxes on Americans making over $400,000 per year, while raising payroll taxes on all working Americans. According to former GOP presidential candidate Rick Santorum, "President Obama got practically everything he wanted—a massive tax hike on over 70% of Americans, and billions more in government spending—as part of a deal negotiated in total secrecy."

Overall, the bill forced the average American to pay $1,257 more in taxes each year. In an obscene twist, the bill included expensive giveaways for Hollywood, Puerto Rico rum producers, NASCAR, and the alternative energy industry.

The bill included a total of 50 tax breaks worth $76 billion for favored industries. According to U.S. Senator John McCain (R-AZ), "It's hard to think of anything that could feed the cynicism of the American people more than larding up the must-pass emergency legislation with giveaways to special interests and campaign contributors."

The problem was that McCain and dozens of other "conservative" Republicans in Congress voted for the bill. To compound this error, House Republicans gave John Boehner another term as Speaker of the House. They rewarded him even though he had been a disaster as Speaker and was a horrible negotiating partner versus President Obama. He was a very ineffective advocate for conservative principles and had purged Tea Party conservatives from key House committees.

This Congressional sellout occurred after a year in which the GOP had lost the presidency while abandoning conservative principles once again. In the aftermath of the 2012 campaign, who could blame voters if they thought there was not much difference between the parties and both were contributing to our problem? Santorum noted that "we have to rally conservatives across America and demand that both Republicans and Democrats slash the federal budget."

Unfortunately, both Democrats and Republicans remained tone deaf to the demands of millions of middle class Americans who were unable to improve their standard of living in a stagnant economy. Although nothing was done to spur economic growth, both parties passed fiscally unsound legislation that added to the national debt and postponed a real discussion of the fiscal crisis.

Santorum believed that "Obama is risking the nation's credit rating with his reckless government spending." Sadly, Republicans were partners in this fiscal crime. A prime example was the fiscal cliff legislation approved by Republican leadership in both houses of Congress.

As Santorum pointed out, "the Republican strategy of 'playing nice' and negotiating with Barack Obama behind closed doors doesn't work. We have to try a new, more aggressive strategy."

Sadly, the House under John Boehner displayed no appetite to address the type of change this country really needed. To move our country forward, the House of Representatives needed to institute real reforms like a balanced budget amendment or Congressional term limits, but Boehner and the leadership team refused to make the tough decisions that our country desperately needed.

Karl Rove, "Bush's Brain," is a Lame Loser

For many years, Fox News viewers have been subjected to hosts welcoming Karl Rove with the title of "The Architect." Supposedly, Rove was this genius consultant who was "Bush's brain" and guided George W. Bush to the White House.

In reality, Rove's candidate lost the popular vote in the 2000 election, barely won re-election against a laughable Democratic candidate, and was routed in the 2006 mid-term elections. In essence, Karl Rove helped usher in Nancy Pelosi as Speaker of the House and Barack Obama as president.

Sadly, he was elevated by Fox News, which used him on a continual basis to comment on political issues. From this high-profile vantage point Rove accumulated $350 million in the 2012 election cycle for his group, American Crossroads. Despite the massive funding, Rove's candidates lost in spectacular fashion. Then Rove added insult to injury by refusing, on national television on Election Night, to acknowledge the Ohio presidential results or Obama's comfortable victory.

This embarrassing performance should have been enough for Fox to permanently ban Rove from their airwaves. Instead, he was signed to another contract. This was a very unfortunate decision by Fox, for the network was the only alternative for many Republicans disgusted by the mainstream news media.

The move showed that Fox was worried about its reputation among the Beltway elite; and sure enough, the network moved to the left after the 2012 election. After deciding to rehire Rove, Fox signed up moderate former GOP Senator Scott Brown and leftist former Congressman Dennis Kucinich. At the same time, Fox decided not to renew the contract of a real conservative contributor, former Alaska Governor Sarah Palin.

Using Fox as his launching pad, Rove was on the airwaves almost every day spouting his RINO nonsense and blasting the Tea Party movement. At the same time, he was trying an "Extreme Makeover," Political Edition. Ludicrously, his new project was named the Conservative Victory Project, an especially ironic moniker in that Karl Rove was not a conservative and was rarely victorious.

With this new project, Rove declared war against the one bright spot in the Republican Party, the Tea Party. He claimed that too many Tea Party candidates had been overly conservative in the last election cycle, and henceforth his group would determine which Republican candidates would be the most electable in GOP primaries. This move smacked of total arrogance and was very heavy-handed. Columnist Bob Woodward likened Rove's new group to the Republican political equivalent of the Politburo.

In fact, this Politburo was about as successful in political campaigns as the Soviet version was in running the Russian economy. In the last election, Rove squandered millions on mostly losing Republican campaigns. In the aftermath, he tried to shift blame to a few Tea Party candidates like Todd Akin who lost after making ill-advised comments. Yet, as noted by Newt Gingrich, Rove's group funded plenty of moderate Republican candidates who were not affiliated with the Tea Party—and still lost in the November 2012 election.

Rove led the GOP to electoral defeats even though the party had the winning formula: promoting real conservative candidates rather than moderate, Country Club Republicans who were, in essence, glorified Democrats.

On the occasions when the party stood firm on true conservative principles, they won historic victories. In the past few decades, the Republican Party has won massive electoral landslides four times: 1980, 1984, 1994 and 2010. In all of those elections, the GOP preached a strong conservative message. In every election where the party has been soundly defeated—1992, 1996, 2006, 2008, and 2012—the party had "moved to the middle."

Despite this, as we have seen, after the Tea Party swept the Republicans to leadership of Congress in 2010, the GOP moved to the left and embraced a very flawed candidate, Mitt Romney. Rove advocated this same strategy going forward; he believed that real conservatism was not electable.

This is a view he has held for many years. In 1976 he supported Gerald Ford instead of Ronald Reagan. In 1980 he supported G.H.W. Bush instead of Reagan. Thus, this "genius" did not support the most consequential conservative the Republican Party ever nominated.

To win the White House in 2016, the GOP must reject Rove's misguided advice, embrace true conservatism, and stand for principle once again.

Bush Library Dedication was a Reminder Why We Miss Reagan

On April 25, 2013, under a clear sky and in front of 10,000 people, all the living members of the most exclusive club in the world gathered in Dallas for the dedication of the George W. Bush presidential Library. It was supposed to be a non-partisan, respectful gathering of former presidents; instead, politics was front and center in the remarks of the Democrats who spoke at the function.

Former president Jimmy Carter used his time to tout George W. Bush's aid to the Sudan and effort to combat AIDS. While these were significant accomplishments and lifesaving, they were relatively minor events in the Bush presidency. Carter said nothing about the honoree's role in the war on terror or his leadership of the country during a very perilous period in our nation's history.

Bill Clinton used his time to make irrelevant remarks, crack jokes, and remind the audience how close he was to the family. It revealed much more about Slick Willy than it did about George W. Bush. For example, only a man who had lied about a relationship with a White House intern could turn presidential library comments into a discussion about naked bathroom paintings.

If Clinton's speech was harmless, if inappropriate, President Obama was utterly political and insulting to his host. He used part of his speech to push for immigration reform. It was not appropriate for Obama to take advantage of a library dedication to tout his personal agenda. Nonetheless, the incident was a reminder of what type of president the country had placed in the White House. For Obama, his role as president was to campaign, not govern; to engage in politics, not show leadership.

It took the Bush family to restore some dignity to the proceedings. George H. W. Bush was in failing health and only spoke for 24 seconds. If he had been able to give a more complete address, it would have surely been marked by class and grace. The honoree, George W. Bush, displayed humility by speaking of what an honor it was to serve as president.

Overall, the gathering was a very sad reflection on the choices the American people had made over the past few decades. Missing at the gathering was president Ronald Reagan, who passed away in 2004. Compared to the men gathered in Dallas, Reagan was a giant, a consequential figure who changed the nation and the world.

By contrast, Carter showed once again why he was a small man who had been a dangerous liberal and a failure as both president and ex-president. The damage he inflicted on the country did not end with his term. He was later employed as an envoy by President Clinton and was completely deceived by the North Koreans, who convinced him that they did not have a nuclear weapons program.

While both Bush Sr. and Bush Jr. possess endearing humility and basic dignity, neither can be considered a successful president. The senior Bush used a "peace dividend" to start dismantling our military, while famously turning back from his commitment not to raise taxes. On the other hand, while George W. Bush was successful in cutting taxes, he also engaged in reckless spending, created a massive new government bureaucracy (the Department of Homeland Security), passed an expensive new entitlement program, and turned a budget surplus into a $468 billion deficit. While displaying resolve in conducting the war on terror, his handling of the wars in Iraq and Afghanistan left much to be desired. Both countries remain mired in the midst of civil wars and beset with terrorists.

In contrast, Reagan's presidency was the model for the nation. He displayed leadership both at home and abroad. He passed historic tax cuts, reignited the economy, created 22 million jobs and ushered in 20 years of economic growth. He restored pride in our country after the disaster of Watergate and the Carter presidency, and rebuilt a crumbling military. His defiance in the face of the communist threat helped end the 70 years of the evil empire, and he brought down the Iron Curtain without firing a shot. Thanks to Reagan, we established a missile defense program that may save this country from an attack by a rogue tyrant in North Korea or Iran.

It is no surprise that recent polls have ranked Reagan as the best president of all time; if he were on the ballot today, he would defeat Obama in a landslide. The Bush library dedication showed us once again what we have missed in presidential leadership and how everything went so wrong in our country.

The Ruination of Rubio

After his rousing keynote address at the 2012 Republican National Convention, U.S. Senator Marco Rubio (R-FL) became the darling of the GOP. A young, articulate, intelligent Cuban-American, Rubio was seen as a leading 2016 presidential candidate. Some commentators even predicted that he was so outstanding he would scare away many of his would-be opponents.

What a difference a year makes! By June of 2013, Rubio was no longer the shining star of the Republican Party, a role that now belonged to U.S. Senators Ted Cruz (R-TX), and Rand Paul (R-KY). Earlier in the year, Rubio had lost some luster when he awkwardly reached for a bottle of water while giving the Republican response to the president's State of the Union speech. He became the butt of jokes from late night comedians and received ridicule on social media, although he retained his positive standing among conservative Republicans, the base of the party.

But a few months later, conservative support for Rubio had evaporated so much that the mere mention of his name caused some Republicans to yell expletives. The reason for the dramatic change was Rubio's strong support for the immigration reform bill.

Right before the July 4th holiday, the Senate passed the bill by a 68-32 margin. The bill included typical pork barrel spending, such as giveaways for the casino industry to help Nevada Senator Harry Reid, special accommodations for the cruise industry to help Rubio's state of Florida, and $1.5 billion for a jobs bill to recruit the support of Vermont Senator Bernie Sanders. The bipartisan group of senators who sponsored the bill was quickly labeled "the Gang of Eight."

The bill, a 1,200-page monstrosity, was loaded with extras, just like the 2,700-page Affordable Care Act of 2010. None of the senators who voted on the bill actually had time to read the entire document or understand everything that was in the legislation.

Tragically, 14 Republican Senators supported the bill, which was sent to the GOP-controlled House of Representatives. Fortunately, conservatives in the House prevented Speaker Boehner from passing the bill. His preference was to tweak the bill and pass his own version, but thankfully he was denied.

All this effort on immigration was a misguided attempt to lure more support from Hispanic voters who had supported Barack Obama in the last election by a 77-23% margin. In their craze to lure Hispanic votes, Republicans forgot about the votes of grass-roots conservatives and Tea Party members who were demanding border security and not amnesty. So it wasn't surprising that Rubio's sky-high approval ratings decreased significantly among self-described conservatives. In a June 2013 Public Policy Poll, his approval rating among "very conservative" respondents declined nine points and among "somewhat conservative" respondents it fell four points. Even among Hispanics, Rubio's approval rating had declined five points since the preceding March. This was quite ironic, for many Republican Party leaders believed that support of the immigration reform bill was essential to build support in the Hispanic community. Well, it didn't work for Senator Rubio, the poster child for the "Gang of Eight."

This motley gang of moderates and liberals included liberal champion New York Senator Chuck Schumer. Most Republicans were appalled that Rubio was pushing a plan supported by not only Schumer, but also President Obama.

It is clear why Democrats such as Obama supported the bill: the moment eleven to 20 million illegal immigrants were given the right to vote, the vast majority would support the Democratic Party. But why did Rubio and other Republican moderates support this bill? While the negative ramifications for the GOP were quite severe, Rubio and company somehow thought that the Republicans would be viewed as pro-Hispanic if the legislation passed. They wanted to be portrayed positively by the critical liberal media, even though the legislation was harmful to both their party and their nation.

In the 2012 presidential election, 77 percent of Hispanic voters cast their ballot for Barack Obama. If the "Gang of Eight" bill had passed, red states like Texas would have turned blue and the GOP would never have a chance to win another presidential election. It seemed as if Rubio had a death wish for the GOP. This was why columnist Ann Coulter called him "the Jack Kevorkian of the Republican party."

Besides the obvious political ramifications, there were many, many reasons for conservatives to oppose the immigration reform bill. One is that it legalized the citizenship of millions of undocumented aliens before giving any consideration to border security. In an interview on Univision, the Spanish language TV network, Rubio said, "First comes the legalization, then come the measures to secure the border, and then comes the process of permanent residence. What we're talking about here is the system of permanent residence. Regarding the legalization, the enormous majority of my colleagues have accepted that it has to happen and that it has to happen at the same time we begin the measures regarding [border] security. It is not conditional. The legalization is not conditional."

This shocking statement contradicted what Rubio had said in other interviews, when he claimed that border security would be implemented before amnesty. It was also not what the American people wanted. By a four-to-one margin, Americans urged that border security be improved before any type of amnesty was granted.

For many years, border security has been a joke. Along the 2,000-mile border with Mexico, only 656 miles of fencing have been completed. It's quite sad to realize that while our country can't build a fence, the Chinese completed a 13,000-mile Great Wall . . . starting in the third century B.C.

Of course, the U.S. government possesses the technology to build a simple fence; it just lacks the political willpower. We have become too concerned with political correctness and how a border fence will be interpreted by our Mexican neighbors and the millions of Hispanic voters in this nation. Thus, we continue to ignore our national security needs, as well as the wishes of the vast majority of Americans.

In supporting immigration reform, Rubio was trying to pander to the mainstream media, the GOP establishment and Hispanic voters. Yet in doing so he threw away the key demographic that controlled the nomination process: grassroots conservatives. After his despicable performance promoting this amnesty bill, conservatives started to rule Rubio out as a presidential candidate.

Finally, after being pummeled on the immigration issue for months, Rubio recanted his position, and by 2015 was on record rejecting "immigration reform" and agreeing with his fellow presidential candidates that border security was needed first. What a politician!

Republicans Facing Revolt

By July of 2013, President Obama was dealing with seven serious scandals and facing a declining public approval rating. It was the perfect opportunity for the GOP to take advantage of his woes, but instead it got up to its usual tricks, snatching defeat from the jaws of victory.

Republicans were in the midst of angering their base and daring grassroots conservatives to form a new party. In fact, former Alaska Governor and 2008 Republican vice presidential candidate Sarah Palin was already considering such a move. In an interview on Fox News, Palin said she liked the idea of forming a Freedom Party with talk show host Mark Levin "if the GOP continues to back away from the planks in our platform, from the principles that built this party of Lincoln and Reagan." Palin believed that the Republican Party ignored conservatives "with that libertarian streak" who want limited government.

In recent years, Republicans had bypassed conservatives and nominated moderate presidential candidates. Despite controlling Congress and the White House during the Bush administration, the government expanded with new entitlement programs and uncontrolled spending. Since January of 2011, the Republicans had controlled the House of Representatives, but were still not successful in stopping the massive spending of the Obama administration. The GOP leadership did nothing to stop the national debt which by that time had surpassed $17 trillion. Despite mandated cuts due to sequester, the annual budget deficit continued to hover around $1 trillion.

To ultimately be successful, the Republican Party needed to serve as a roadblock to stop the liberal Democrats; otherwise, there was nothing to prevent reckless spending and the continual growth of government. Unfortunately, Republicans continued to pander to certain demographic groups and be politically correct and did not stop the Democrats from inflicting severe fiscal damage to the country.

They ignored the sage advice of the late Scottish chaplain Peter Marshall who once said, "If you don't stand for something, you'll fall for anything." At this point, there were very few Republicans who stood on principle, regardless of the political consequences.

The Race Begins: Paul vs. Christie

By late July of 2013, the GOP presidential race for 2016 had already begun. The first shot was fired at a Republican Governor's forum in Aspen, Colorado, where New Jersey Governor Chris Christie blasted Libertarians as "very dangerous." The Governor noted his troubles with the spread of libertarianism in both political parties, specifically targeting U.S. Senator Rand Paul.

At the time, Christie was on his way to winning re-election as Governor of New Jersey and was preparing a campaign for president in 2016. He knew very well that one of his challengers for the nomination would likely be Senator Paul.

Christie represented the old school, big government Republican philosophy embodied by the previous two GOP presidential nominees, John McCain and Mitt Romney. Paul, on the other hand, represented a much different philosophy embraced by the growing wing of the party that was disgusted with the elitists who control the GOP. This group included Libertarians, Tea Party activists and conservative Republicans who for decades had been denied leadership roles in the party.

Since the 1960s, the moderate country club, elitist wing of the Republican Party had been in charge. The results have been devastating as the GOP lost the popular vote in five of the last six presidential elections. Only two conservatives in the last five decades were able to take control of the Republican Party: Barry Goldwater in 1964 and Ronald Reagan in 1980 and 1984.

As a moderate, Christie was similar to all of those losing GOP presidential candidates; he was on the wrong side of history. He was also on the wrong side of the issues. RINO politicians like Christie approved of only a little less government spending than Democrats. True conservatives like Paul wanted to actually reduce the size and scope of the government. While Christie was a big supporter of NSA surveillance of innocent Americans, Paul wanted to limit this type of oppressive government monitoring that had been expanding in recent years.

Not only did Christie believe that the government needed to collect data from innocent Americans to keep the country safe, he was a strong supporter of all of Obama's counterterrorism policies. According to Christie, "President Obama has done nothing to change the policies of the Bush administration in the war on terrorism. And I mean practically nothing. And you know why? 'Cause they work."

The policies that Christie embraced included the TSA groping travelers in airports and the NSA illegally spying on millions of innocent Americans. In addition, he endorsed the expansion of the Department of Homeland Security, which was supposedly created to coordinate the federal government's war against terrorism, but was actually nothing more than a massive new government bureaucracy that represented yet another way to grow government and infringe on the freedoms of Americans.

Governor Christie obviously did understand that our privacy was under constant assault from the government, all in the name of fighting terrorism. Senator Paul understood that a surveillance state was very dangerous, very Orwellian. It was not consistent with our U.S. Constitution, nor was it consistent with the values of everyday Americans. According to Paul, "Christie worries about the dangers of freedom. I worry about the danger of losing that freedom. Spying without warrants is unconstitutional."

Not only was Christie wrong on the issue of national security, he was wrong on fiscal issues. The Governor was typical of the big government mentality that had created the ever-growing national debt. His philosophy fueled the mess we face today. Rand Paul offered a new approach—conservatism—and understood that the government was already too large, and any expansion of government surveillance was dangerous.

Like many Northeastern Republicans, Christie was very cozy with Democrats like Obama and Clinton. He tried to do business with the Democrats. He also agreed with the Democrats on too many vital issues, and in the previous election had provided President Obama with a big boost by lavishing inappropriate praise on the president for his handling of Hurricane Sandy. Christie insisted that Obama, who came around for a few photo opportunities with storm victims, had provided inspirational leadership and helped the region recover. In reality, Christie might have been trying to sabotage the campaign of Mitt Romney while helping Obama win, and thereby creating a wide-open presidential race in 2016. His actions were more likely politically motivated than anything else.

In contrast, Rand Paul opposed Democrats. For example, during the Benghazi hearings he plainly told Hillary Clinton that she should have been relieved of her command as Secretary of State for her "dereliction" of duty during the September 11, 2012 terrorist attack. Paul represented a break with the past, a return to a Goldwater type of nominee who was not afraid to take on the establishment within his own party and in the federal government.

The real danger was not the philosophy espoused by Paul and many other true conservatives; it was the toxic, politics-as-usual philosophy aptly represented by one of the liberals' favorite Republicans: Governor Chris Christie.

GOP Leadership Continued to Disappoint

In early September of 2013, polls consistently showed that the vast majority of Americans were opposed to military intervention in Syria. In Congressional offices, calls were running 100 to one against U.S. involvement in Syria. Nevertheless, leaders of both political parties supported the president's plan to launch a limited military strike in Syria.

It was politically understandable that leaders of the Democratic Party would stand behind a Democrat president. However, it was inconceivable that Republican leaders like House Speaker John

Boehner (R-OH) and Majority Leader Eric Cantor (R-VA) would also give President Obama political cover.

Once again the Republican Party had lost its way. The party was not united; there was a massive fight between the libertarian and establishment wings. Unfortunately, the leadership of the GOP was firmly aligned with the latter. On issue after issue, moderate Republicans were never in favor of making drastic changes to our federal government. Instead, they wanted to get along with the Democrats, curry favor with the media, and retain their positions of power.

On the issue of Syria, libertarians and conservatives initially questioned why our country was getting involved in that country's civil war. It was a nasty war in which chemical weapons had been launched, but there was conflicting evidence regarding who had been behind the attack.

Questions remained: What was our national security interest in Syria, and who were these rebels that the U.S. administration wanted to support? The opposition to the Assad regime was composed of many different organizations, including terrorists linked to Al Qaeda and the organization that eventually came to be known as the Islamic State.

Videos were released showing so-called moderate rebels beheading Catholic priests, eating the hearts and livers of Syrian soldiers, and executing Assad supporters in cold blood. The United States should never have considered supporting cannibals, terrorists and anti-Christian extremists.

It was not just the Syrian war in which grassroots Republicans were on one side and the GOP leadership on the other. Whether the issue was taxes, de-funding Obamacare, NSA spying, or Syria, the leadership of the Republican Party did the bidding of bureaucrats and special interests, not the grassroots.

The GOP leadership was disconnected from the people who

volunteer, donate and allow the party to win elections. They were supporting a party that was a captive of the Beltway, rather than representing their interests. Republicans just needed to listen to their constituents. Even war hawk U.S. Senator John McCain (R-AZ) received an earful from his voters at town hall meetings, but the same thing was happening all over the country.

Regarding Syria, the House and Senate intelligence committees approved CIA weapons shipments to the "rebels," only to see all non-lethal aid revoked in December of 2013 amidst concerns that the Islamic State was stealing the aid and using it to expand their territorial gains. Eventually, in September 2014, arms shipments to and training of the rebels was approved by Congress, but for only a few months because of growing anxiety that the aid was helping the Islamic State instead of the so-called "moderate rebels." Thereafter, the aid continued with limited results, and has been enhanced by limited air strikes from the U.S. and various allies targeting Islamic State strongholds. Still, despite the additional U.S. involvement, Syria, like Libya, is a failed state with various terrorist groups in control; the Obama administration has only exacerbated problems in both countries.

Jeb Bush Disqualified for GOP Nomination

The day before the 12-year anniversary of the 9/11 terrorist attacks and the one-year anniversary of the Benghazi terror attack, former Florida Governor Jeb Bush showed his true colors.

Bush gave the "Liberty Medal" to former Secretary of State Hillary Clinton at the annual ceremony sponsored by the National Constitution Center. Previous winners of this award included

Supreme Court Justice Thurgood Marshall, U.N. Secretary General Kofi Annan, and rock star Bono, which clearly indicated the organization's hard-left tilt.

Being involved in presenting this award should have forever disqualified Bush from consideration for the GOP presidential nomination. He was Chairman of the Board of Trustees for the National Constitutional Center, and very much involved with this liberal group that gave such a prestigious award to Hillary Clinton, an individual who was clearly undeserving. It showed that Bush was comfortable being a tool of liberals and instead of confronting them in the arena of ideas, he was bestowing an honor on one of their cherished heroines.

According to Bush, Clinton deserved the award because she "dedicated her life to serving and engaging people across the world in democracy. These efforts as a citizen, an activist, and a leader have earned Secretary Clinton this year's Liberty Medal."

Of course Clinton deserved an award for liberalism, not liberty. Throughout her career she has advocated big government, the enemy of all liberty lovers. The National Constitution Center should have realized that Clinton has encouraged the shredding of the Constitution for years. She had even advocated socialized medicine long before Obama was able to pass his misguided and unworkable program.

In foreign policy, Clinton had been a disaster in dealing with Russia and the Arab Spring uprisings in Libya, Egypt, Syria and other hotspots across the world. Her worst scandal involved her outrageous conduct regarding the terrorist attack in Benghazi, which merited her not the "Liberty" medal, but the "Liberal Liar" medal.

Clinton did nothing to protect the Americans under siege in Benghazi, and in the aftermath of the attack she lied to the American people and blamed the violence on an Internet video. In testimony before Congress, Clinton famously asked, regarding why the Americans were killed, "What difference does it make?" This chilling, evil statement not only insulted the friends and families of the four Americans killed in the Benghazi attack, but every justice-loving individual in this country.

It made a big difference why these Americans were killed. We deserved the truth about what happened and why, in order to make sure that this type of attack never occurs again. It made a big difference that Clinton told falsehoods to the American people about an incident that led to the deaths of four people, including the U.S. Ambassador. Incredibly, after all this time, only one terrorist has been captured and held responsible for this attack, and Americans still do not know exactly what transpired on that fateful night.

It was shameful that Bush gave this award to Clinton on the eve of the Benghazi anniversary. It showed that he was either tone deaf on the issue or did not care about the legitimate concerns Americans felt regarding Clinton's behavior during the Benghazi attack. By rewarding Clinton for her lies, Bush should have been disqualified from consideration for the 2016 GOP presidential nomination and not even bothered to run his rather inept, poorly managed and pathetic campaign.

As noted by Barbara Bush—the former First Lady and Jeb's mother—there are plenty of people qualified to run for president in 2016, and the country has "had enough Bushes." Well said, Mrs. Bush. It's obvious that mother knows best.

Cruz Stands for America

By the beginning of the fall in 2013, the American people were witnessing the emergence of a new star on the political scene: U.S. Senator Ted Cruz (R-TX). He captivated millions of Americans with his amazing 21-hour filibuster against Obamacare.

While dinosaurs in the media and the U.S. Senate raised objections to this noble crusade, the majority of the American people rejoiced that someone was finally standing up for them. Cruz stated that politicians needed to "listen" to their constituents, a foreign concept to most politicians in Washington, D.C. Establishment Senators, both Democrat and Republican, obviously did not read poll results. Since the inception of Obamacare, Americans have consistently registered their strong opposition to this government takeover of the healthcare industry, which constitutes almost one-fifth of our economy.

As Cruz was leading the filibuster against Obamacare, a poll by NBC and the *Wall Street Journal* showed that by a two-to-one margin, 45-23 percent, Americans believed that Obamacare would have a negative impact on the country's health care system. During his filibuster, Cruz represented these frustrated Americans who were petrified about Obamacare, a law that eventually led to higher health insurance premiums, a shortage of medical care and an uncertain future for the healthcare industry.

While Cruz was leading the lonely filibuster, the old guard in the U.S. Senate were furious. They were upset that the good old boy system of politics-as-usual was being challenged. John McCain and Mitch McConnell, who collectively had almost six decades of Senate experience, led the charge against Cruz, who had been elected only the previous November. Their outrageous behavior was embarrassing and exposed once again the wisdom of term limits on Capitol Hill.

Is it Time for Conservatives to File for Divorce from the GOP?

By mid-October of 2013, the fallout from the government shutdown debacle had proven devastating for the Republican Party. Poll results showed that the party was viewed negatively by 70% of the American people with Congress at only a 5% approval rating, the lowest in history. Although the filibuster was a principled attempt to stop a horrific program from being implemented, it was demonized by fellow Republicans and the media eagerly joined the fray. While Democrats controlled the Senate and were also unpopular, the media focused their blame for the shutdown on the Republican Party.

At the same time, President Obama's approval rating of 37% was the lowest of his presidency. If a Republican president had suffered from such poor poll numbers, the media would have been in a frenzied state, but such was not the case with Obama. The media decided to spend all of their time lambasting the Republican Party.

As usual, the Republicans did a poor job of defending their principled opposition to Obamacare and the rest of the Obama agenda. Most GOP leaders lacked basic communication skills. They had a compelling story to tell about how Obamacare would be harmful to the economy and the healthcare industry, but they did not possess the ability to break through media bias. Throughout the shutdown drama, Republicans offered five different compromise proposals and a multitude of specific spending bills to target critical areas of the budget, all to no avail. Democrats refused to budge from their position that Obamacare could not be delayed.

The House Republicans initially wanted to defund Obamacare completely, but that position later morphed into a call for individuals to be given a one-year exemption from the plan, the same benefit offered to businesses. This proposal was quite reasonable, but the Congressional Republican leadership had difficulty selling their position to the American people.

One major problem was the constant criticism from within their own ranks. Senator John McCain and others were relentless in blaming Senators Ted Cruz and Mike Lee for the government shutdown. Instead of supporting fellow Republicans for embarking on such a noble cause, the old guard Republicans threw their colleagues under the bus.

The criticism scared House Speaker Boehner, who eventually called for a grand compromise that raised the debt ceiling, funded the government and basically forgot about fighting Obamacare. The proposal was a shell of their original position; instead of calling for the end of the entire Obamacare program, it only offered to eliminate the medical device tax, thus negating the two-week battle over the President's cherished program.

As usual, Boehner caved in to the President and the Democrats, giving conservatives one more reason to hate the Republican Party leadership. This debate reminded everyone that the Republican Party remained hopelessly controlled by its moderate, establishment wing; conservatives were clearly on the outside. If they took bold positions like Cruz had, they would be demonized by RINOs, Democrats and the media alike.

Once again, the saga led conservatives to question their marriage to the Republican Party. Some wanted to file divorce papers on the GOP, citing irreconcilable differences.

In fact, after the government shutdown debate, the third party position had the support of plenty of Americans. A mid-October 2013 Gallup poll showed that 60% of citizens favored the creation of a major third party. This was the strongest sentiment for a third party that Gallup has registered in the 10-year history of the poll question.

Mitch McConnell, Ringside Politics Turkey of the Year 2013

Every Thanksgiving, all of us at Ringside Politics decide who is most deserving of our Turkey of the Year Award. Twenty-thirteen was another great year for turkeys—not the poultry variety, but the politicians, celebrities, athletes and entertainers who engaged in outrageous behavior. Unlike most honors, our award is not coveted, for the honoree should hold his or her head in shame. The winner is someone who engaged in especially dumb behavior, befitting of the pea brained fowl we carve up each year at the holiday dinner table.

Past winners of this shameful honor include blowhard film-maker Michael Moore; corrupt former New Orleans Mayor Ray Nagin; and the queen of perks and privilege, former House Speaker Nancy Pelosi.

It is always a difficult decision, but 2013 was especially challenging since Americans had been exposed to so many people who qualified. Nevertheless, after an arduous decision- making process, and considering many truly qualified candidates, the 2013 Ringside Politics Turkey of the Year was bestowed upon U.S. Senator Mitch McConnell (R-KY).

At the time, McConnell was the Senate Minority Leader. Known for his anti-Tea Party views, he was upset because the Tea Party and other true conservatives wanted to shake up Capitol Hill. He even claimed that he wanted to punch one Tea Party group in the nose. He was also the poster child for term limits, as he has served in the U.S. Senate since 1985 and was running for a sixth term at the age of 71.

McConnell spent his career acting like a disengaged, arrogant politician who believed that he was indispensable to our nation. One of the many reasons that Washington D. C. is always broken is that the politicians who created the problems in the first place are still there trying to "fix" them. Our Founders never envisioned a country in which so many politicians make public service into a full-time career.

In 2014, McConnell survived a Tea Party primary challenge and won re-election. The following January he was elected Senate Majority Leader, fulfilling the worst nightmare of every true conservative. He used his position to pursue big government policies, more spending, as well as funding for Obamacare and the president's executive decision to grant amnesty to five million illegal aliens. Sadly, none of this was unexpected once the voters of Kentucky rejected new leadership and re-elected a familiar politician with name recognition, big money, and no incentive to change the way Washington D.C. works.

McConnell has always typified the old guard: a Senator comfortable with the politics-as-usual arrangement that has destroyed our economy and our political climate. Not surprisingly, he detested the tactics of Ted Cruz, especially the filibuster Cruz led to remove funding for Obamacare. Not surprisingly, McConnell believed the filibuster was a misguided attempt to de-fund Obamacare, and the resulting shutdown was a disaster. At a retreat with big donors and lobbyists at the ritzy Sea Island, GA resort, McConnell vowed to never allow another shutdown.

He declared war on the Tea Party and the Ted Cruz-led, anti-establishment wing of the U.S. Senate. McConnell hated Cruz and company for challenging his ineffective leadership tactics. In reality,

Cruz had exposed the dangers of Obamacare, and Americans had started to see how damaging this "health care reform" was to our country. Unlike McConnell, Cruz performed a great service to the American people.

Compared to Obamacare, the government shutdown was a walk in the park. Thousands of government employees were furloughed during the shutdown, but they later returned to their jobs with full pay, no harm, no foul. In contrast, Obamacare was already generating horrific damage as millions of Americans received health insurance cancellation notices. When many of these people were able to find new insurance, they faced higher health insurance costs.

While he was incensed at Cruz, McConnell did absolutely nothing when then-Majority Leader Harry Reid (D-NV) pushed through the "nuclear option," an amazing power play to fast track Obama appointments. This move eviscerated the GOP minority by eliminating the 200 plus-year history of the filibuster for executive and judicial nominees other than the Supreme Court. The end result of this decision was a further limitation on the power of Republican Senators. It showed how McConnell was comfortable being played the fool by Reid and President Obama.

As Democrats engaged in brass-knuckle tactics, McConnell pursued compromise and the conciliatory Senate rules of a bygone era. He reserved his anger not for liberal Democratic colleagues but for Republican conservatives. The result: As McConnell negotiated and yielded on conservative principles, liberals made consistent gains.

In a fall 2013 interview with the Lexington *Herald-Leader*, McConnell bragged of his record of deal-making with Vice president Joe Biden. Unfortunately, this history of compromise and concession only conveyed weakness to the Democrats and the American people.

It was politicians like Mitch McConnell who created the obscenely high national debt and a federal government that continues to grow and become more intrusive. It is time for a new approach to solve our ongoing crises. McConnell had his chance. He failed, so he needs to exit from leadership.

Good riddance to this turkey. Republicans must offer *true* conservatism in 2016; it's their only chance of victory.

VI

2014

Time for the GOP to Listen to the American People

By January of 2014, the House GOP leadership was preparing to take action on the immigration issue. According to reports, proposed legislation included "principles" of immigration reform and a "pathway" to citizenship for the estimated 12 million illegal immigrants in our country. This bill reportedly included a mandate to improve border security, provide additional visas for foreign workers, and require those immigrants seeking legalization to learn English and pay certain fees.

The net effect of this legislation would have been "amnesty" for millions of immigrants who had ignored our laws to settle in this country. It was a way of rewarding lawbreakers while insulting the 1.2 million individuals who deal each year with the arduous process of legally becoming a citizen. This process should be expanded only if our country needs to import a larger talent pool of workers in certain types of industries, such as healthcare.

House GOP leaders claimed that action was needed on immigration since it was supposedly a pressing issue impacting the country. However, poll numbers showed that Americans were much more concerned about other matters. In fact, according to a January 2014 Gallup poll, only 3% of Americans listed immigration reform as a top priority for 2014.

According to Gallup's Lydia Saad, 21% of respondents listed "the government" itself as the most serious problem facing the country. The economy was ranked as the second most important problem, followed by unemployment/jobs and healthcare. Americans also cited foreign aid, the debt and deficit, poverty, income inequality and ethics in government as much more important issues than immigration reform. Nevertheless, Washington politicians were keen to move ahead on immigration legislation, taking their marching orders from special interest groups such as the Chamber of Commerce and various Hispanic advocacy organizations.

Immigration legislation was also supported by big business interests, influential in the GOP because it allowed for the cheap foreign labor to be continually recruited. On the other side of the fence, it also provided Democrats with a steady stream of loyal voters. In the last presidential election, Barack Obama enjoyed the support of 73% of Hispanic voters.

Unfortunately, history made it clear that any immigration deal would only lead to more illegal immigration in the future, such as when three million immigrants were given amnesty in 1986. Offering legal status to millions of undocumented workers always displaces more Americans from jobs as well as adding to the pool of 102 million Americans who are either unemployed or not participating in the labor force. Those outside of the labor force include retirees and also those who are so despondent that they have given up looking for work and are living on their savings, on government assistance or literally on the streets, homeless.

Fortunately, some House Republicans were not silent about the danger involved in this issue. A 16-member GOP group led by U.S. Congressman Mo Brooks (R-AL) wrote an urgent letter to President Obama warning that "Rapidly expanding unskilled immigration–at a time when factory work and blue collar jobs are disappearing–would represent the final economic blow for millions of workers who have been struggling to gain an economic foothold." Representative Brooks had his priorities in the right order. More of our leaders should be focused on ways to help struggling Americans rather than rewarding those illegal immigrants who have ignored our laws.

It was a tragedy that so many Republican leaders supported amnesty legislation for illegal aliens that decreased job opportunities and the standard of living for law abiding American citizens, who suffered the most under the Obama economy and had few, if any, political leaders concerned about their plight.

One Republican Finally Takes the Gloves Off

By mid-2014 it was clear that the IRS, under the direction of the disgraced Lois Lerner, had targeted Tea Party groups for enhanced scrutiny. This tactic made a mockery of the organization's supposed non-partisanship and objectivity.

With a scandal of this magnitude, the Republicans should have been holding prime time televised hearings and clamoring for a Special Prosecutor. However, those are the tactics of Democrats, who know how to play hardball politics; it is in their blood. Usually, Republicans act like ladies and gentlemen and prefer to stay within the rules and show proper etiquette. As a result, they continued to be rolled over by the more aggressive Democrats.

Fortunately, every once in a great while a Republican displays some justified outrage over corruption and abuse within the federal government. This was certainly warranted in the scandal involving the IRS targeting Tea Party groups for selective scrutiny. Some of these conservative groups were forced to submit to numerous audits while others had their non-profit applications needlessly delayed. The IRS did not use the same tactics with liberal groups according to a Congressional investigation, so bias most certainly played a role.

In the June 20, 2014 hearing of the House Ways and Means Committee, Representative Paul Ryan (R-WI) accused IRS Commissioner John Koskinen of lying. "I am sitting here listening to this testimony. I just–I don't believe it.... Nobody believes you," Ryan said.

From the beginning of the investigation into allegations that the agency improperly targeted Tea Party groups, the IRS was less than forthcoming. First they claimed that no targeting occurred, and that liberal groups were subjected to the same scrutiny. Then it was disclosed that the targeting was the work of some "rogue" agents in the Cincinnati field office. All of these claims were eventually proven to be false.

The week before the hearing, the IRS hid in a 27-page letter the bombshell revelation that the computer hard drive of disgraced former IRS official Lois Lerner had crashed and been "recycled." Her emails from 2009-2011 were supposedly lost forever, along with the emails of six other IRS officials.

This revelation was too much for Ryan, who noted that the emails had been requested the previous May. The IRS said that the crash had been discovered in February of 2014, and the White House learned of it two months later. But it was another two months before the IRS decided to inform the entity that was investigating their activities, the House of Representatives.

To say the situation smelled to high heaven would be the understatement of the century. The Lerner emails were critical to determine whether she had been directing the IRS mistreatment of Tea Party organizations under orders from the White House or other administration officials. With the revelation of the computer crash, the real truth was the true casualty.

Clearly, there was an urgent need for a special prosecutor to be appointed. No one of any integrity could place trust in the president's henchman, Attorney General Eric Holder, to investigate wrongdoing in the administration. The problem, of course, was that a special prosecutor investigating the Executive Branch could be appointed only by the Attorney General, who would never allow justice to supersede politics.

Even though Lerner's computer had supposedly been "recycled," the emails could have been retrieved another way—through the National Security Agency. According to NSA whistleblower William Binney, the agency had recorded all electronic communication since 2001. The Lerner emails might therefore be contained in one of their massive facilities, like the Utah Data Center. Of course, the problem with this course of action was that the president would have to direct the NSA to release the information—and he would never willingly put his administration in such peril.

It was up to members of Congress like Paul Ryan to keep the pressure on the IRS and the Obama administration about this matter. The woman at the center of the scandal, Lois Lerner, was in contempt of Congress for refusing to testify about her role in the scandal. Congress could have used their Constitutional authority to have her arrested and placed in the Capitol jail—but of course Republicans never took such bold action.

The same process should have been used on all the IRS and Obama administration officials who refused to cooperate with the investigation. Only that type of dramatic action would have gotten the attention of the individuals trying to cover up this scandal.

To get to the truth, Congress should have taken the lead of Paul Ryan and turned the tables on the IRS and the Obama White House. Sadly, Ryan's outburst was not followed up by concrete action, and the complete story of how the IRS targeted Tea Party groups was never revealed to the public. This is another example of Republicans fumbling a golden opportunity to use the power at their disposal to put pressure on their political opponents.

Inert Congress Plays Role of Obama Lap Dog

In early August of 2014, Congress was getting ready to embark on another extravagant and wasteful five-week vacation. The president was readying his family for their annual 16 day Martha's Vineyard summer trip. This annual vacation gives the Obama family a chance to luxuriate in a five-star resort, and the president more opportunities to enjoy his favorite activities, such as biking and golfing.

No one knows the full extent of Vice president Joe Biden's summer vacation, but no doubt it included skinny dipping. According to Ron Kessler in his book *The First Family Detail*, Biden enjoyed naked swimming, to the consternation of the female Secret Service agents assigned to protect him.

At any rate, while the politicians were getting ready to have fun, the world was literally in flames. The Ukraine civil war was raging, the conflict between Israel and Hamas remained deadly, and an Ebola epidemic was spreading in Africa.

On the home front, our border was being overrun, and the president's only solution was to demand more money. The crisis forced then-Texas Governor Rick Perry to take action, supplementing official Border Patrol agents with 1,000 members of his National Guard.

The economy also remained stagnant, with anemic job growth reported in July. Only 209,000 jobs had been created, fewer than economists predicted. More importantly, over 92 million Americans remained outside the work force, and the labor force participation rate registered an anemic level of 62.9%. Those lucky Americans with jobs faced stagnant wages while inflation continued to loom on the horizon.

Overall, it was a very perilous time for our top political leaders to start extended vacations. Of course that did not matter to politicians, who are accustomed to working very little while being rewarded very handsomely. But since they were skipping work in August, did Americans really need them to return in the fall? What good did they do anyway?

The Senate under Harry Reid did almost nothing, and the House under John Boehner was not much better. They refused to pass term limits legislation, a balanced budget amendment, real tax relief, or to demand that current laws on border security and illegal immigration be enforced. Instead, their answer was to spend money we did not have, increasing the deficit and plunging the nation into more debt that was by then approaching $18 trillion. To make matters worse, Obamacare persisted as a national disaster, an unconstitutional power grab Congress refused to defund.

The problem was that Speaker Boehner did not actually believe in conservatism. He was a raging moderate masquerading as a conservative. If he had had his way, the House would have passed immigration reform, granting de facto amnesty to the 12-plus million illegal aliens in the country.

At the time, with House conservatives blocking immigration reform, there was talk that President Obama would unilaterally grant amnesty and give work permits to millions of illegal aliens.

Some conservative activists believed such a move would have merited impeachment—a concept Boehner called a "scam."

In reality, it wouldn't have been a scam to impeach Obama for breaking the law, trashing the Constitution, violating the separation of powers, and ordering an executive action to grant amnesty. Impeachment should have been a viable threat to prevent Obama from running roughshod over a Congress that liberal Constitutional professor Jonathan Turley called "inert."

Instead, we were treated to a do-nothing, inert Congress that was terrified of the media and the president, and unwilling to tackle the real problems facing our country. The true "scam" was that John Boehner got re-elected Speaker of the House and led a Congress that was becoming irrelevant as the executive branch assumed ever more power.

Of course, at the time, the 2014 mid-term elections loomed large. There was still hope that the American people would rise up and elect a new Congress: one with courage, common sense and an interest in getting to work, not just going on recess.

Sadly, such hopes were a pipe dream. The new Congress displayed more of the same: cowardice, selfishness, and a continuation of the corrupt game of politics as usual.

Republican Party Insanity

*Insanity: doing the same thing over and over
again and expecting different results.*
—Albert Einstein

By late August of 2014, political insiders started to look ahead to the 2016 presidential race. Unbelievably, the drumbeat was beginning for former Massachusetts Governor Mitt Romney to run for president a third time. The man who had lost twice for president was being encouraged by many party leaders to give it another try. Congressman Jason Chaffetz (R-UT) told MSNBC, "I think he's proven right on a lot of stuff. I happen to be in the camp that thinks he's actually going to run and I think he'll be the next president of the United States."

Chaffetz was not alone; commentator Ann Coulter, Internet titan Matt Drudge and many others were also pushing Romney to run in 2016. In fact, Congressman Paul Ryan, the Governor's running mate in 2012, told reporters that he would "love to see Mitt Romney run for president again."

Despite still being the darling of the establishment wing of the Republican party and continuing to hold a well-deserved reputation as a flip-flopper, Romney was positioned to defeat Barack Obama in the last election. He won the first debate and only needed strong performances in the final two outings to seal the deal with the American people. Instead, he listened to advisers and played it safe. The result: he missed many opportunities to blast the president on the Benghazi debacle and wound up agreeing with Obama on a number of issues.

In the 2012 election, his comments about the "47%" of Americans on government assistance or his remarks about "binders full of women" were misinterpreted by voters. His successful background as a Bain Capital executive was easy fodder for Democrats to attack him as a rich, heartless businessman. Alas, his leadership position in the Mormon Church was an issue for some evangelical Christian voters who were not comfortable supporting a candidate who did not share their religious faith.

In other words, for reasons both fair and unfair, Mitt Romney had not been a particularly good presidential candidate in the previous two elections. Nevertheless, insiders in the Republican Party were in love with the idea of another Romney campaign.

According to Ryan, Romney in 2016 made sense because "the third time's the charm."

Fortunately, Romney didn't take the bait. Initially he was adamant that he would not run at all, then he started to consider it seriously; but eventually he bowed out of the race—the right decision, for Romney would never have been able to win. Thankfully, he realized himself that it was time for the Republican Party to start a new chapter.

The 2016 chapter needs to feature a nominee who can articulate a positive message to the American people and who is a reliable conservative. Only a conservative Republican can win in 2016. Let's hope and pray that Republican primary voters recognize this undeniable truth and select a winning candidate, not another loser in the mold of Mitt Romney.

Republican Party Cowards

The 2014 mid-term elections were a resounding victory for the Republican Party, as the GOP took back control of the Senate and added to their majority in the House. Nonetheless, the victory was not due to Republicans taking tough stances on key issues. Instead, the whole campaign was based on an anti-President Obama message. While this strategy worked, it did not give Republicans a unifying platform on which to rally the country. In 2014 there was nothing to match the Contract with America.

Thus, in the immediate aftermath of the election, the president was extremely provocative with the GOP. After getting shellacked in the mid-terms, Obama did not move to the middle or reach out to Republicans—he moved further to the political left.

After meetings with Congressional Democrats (but no Republicans,) the president announced his long-awaited plan for executive amnesty, giving five million illegal immigrants a pathway to work permits and relief from possible deportation for three years.

It was an audacious announcement, both purely unconstitutional and needlessly confrontational. It totally circumvented Congress, one of the three branches of government, and was radically different from the last time amnesty had been given to illegal immigrants. In 1986, President Reagan did not issue an executive decision on illegal immigration; he signed a bill passed by Congress.

Sadly, this president once again showed his contempt for Congress. Ever since his initial election, he had expressed no desire to meet or work with Republicans in Congress. In fact, his actions were those of an out-of-control president, hell-bent on accumulating executive power rather than acting in conjunction with Congress.

In response, Congress had several options, such as impeachment, lawsuits, or simply defunding all the activities associated with this executive action. The least attractive option was to do nothing—but that was what happened when Congressional Republicans boarded planes and left town for their Thanksgiving vacation.

In the face of a "Constitutional crisis" and a lawless president's unprecedented executive action, the GOP acted like cowards. While House Speaker John Boehner said the House "will act" and that Barack Obama was "damaging the presidency," he offered no specific response. This was especially pitiful because Boehner and the GOP leadership had known for weeks that Obama was going to make this announcement after the mid-term election.

Instead of fighting, Speaker Boehner and incoming Senate Majority Leader Mitch McConnell fled Capitol Hill—the response of cowards. Of course, Republican leaders were afraid of disturbing their big business benefactors, who love cheap labor and who applauded the president's action. In addition, they were afraid of being called nasty names by Democrat leaders, the president, Hispanic activists and the liberal media.

They only group the GOP leadership was not afraid of insulting was comprised of the grassroots conservatives in their own party. They did not hesitate to clash with those good patriotic Americans, the backbone of the GOP. They played the role of pathetic lap dog with the president and his liberal supporters.

Conservatives who were looking for a champion did not find one in McConnell or Boehner. Nor did they find one in 2016 amongst the establishment presidential candidates, such as New Jersey Governor Chris Christie or former Florida Governor Jeb Bush who both failed to generate much support and dropped out of the race.

Fortunately, this election does offer some unique and courageous "outsider" candidates such as businessman Donald Trump and U.S. Senator Ted Cruz who are generating voter support. However, if the Republican Party as a political organization does not start positively responding to grassroots conservatives, these key activists will eventually bolt the GOP.

Even after the 2014 mid-term elections, the GOP Congress refused to stand up to President Obama and stop key components of his agenda from being funded and implemented. In fact the president sprinted further to the left by signing a new climate change agreement limiting our carbon emissions, appointing a very liberal Attorney General, and offering a bold plan to increase government oversight of the Internet, to name only a few. All of those initiatives were threats to this country, but were not met with an aggressive, confident and clear GOP response.

Of course, the biggest insult came when the president announced his executive action on illegal immigration. Twenty-six states, led by Texas, sued the president—but the cowardly Republican Congress never did anything about it.

John Boehner Wins Ringside Politics Turkey of the Year Award

After 2014, a year of some hits but plenty of misses, we again had tough time deciding who was the most qualified for the Ringside Politics Turkey of the Year Award. As usual, we had plenty of nominees to consider, but after an especially difficult selection process, the winner was clear: Republican Speaker of the House John Boehner. When Mr. Boehner was not crying during an interview, tanning at the salon, or playing golf with Barack Obama, he was "leading" Congressional Republicans.

It is an embarrassment that Boehner was the most powerful Republican in the country in 2014. Speaker Boehner was third in line to the presidency, but he did not exude any confidence or leadership ability. He continued to act like a dyed-in-the-wool member of the establishment, who often showed his hatred for the Tea Party.

As Speaker, Boehner displayed no courage, principles or political instincts. Despite the overwhelming Republican victory in November of 2014 and the president's unconstitutional executive amnesty order, Speaker Boehner abdicated his authority and left for Thanksgiving vacation. It took almost two years for a special house committee to be established to investigate the Benghazi attack. When Attorney General Eric Holder refused to provide Congress the needed documents on the Fast and Furious investigation and former IRS official Lois Lerner refused to cooperate on the charges her agency harassed Tea Party groups, both were held in Contempt of Congress. Unfortunately, nothing else happened to either transgressor.

When the president expanded executive power to grant amnesty to 5 million illegal immigrants, Boehner did nothing. Ever since losing the mid-term elections, the president became emboldened, acting aggressively on a range of issues from climate change to government oversight of the Internet. All of these initiatives were threats to this country and should have been met with a confident and clear GOP response as well as a close examination of all political and legal remedies. In reality, nothing was done by Boehner.

While the Republicans won the mid-term elections, they acted like the losers, while the big loser, President Obama, acted like the winner. While Boehner advised caution, Obama started swinging for the fences. Republicans won the mid-term because Americans wanted the GOP to stop the Obama agenda, not roll over and play dead. Boehner showed toughness only against conservatives in his own party.

Certainly, there was some buyers' remorse among conservatives who saw rhetoric, but no action, from GOP leaders. For example, in the mid-term races, many Republican candidates campaigned on the illegal immigration issue, claiming they would stop amnesty. Yet, efforts to eliminate funding for executive amnesty were opposed by Boehner and House GOP leaders. They claimed they did not have the power to deny funding. Baloney, according to U.S. Senator Jeff Sessions (R-AL), who asserted that Congress had the power to remove funding. In the end, nothing was done, a very familiar story.

Boehner did not act because he was worried about a government shutdown and was too afraid of the Republican Party's big business donors who demanded cheap labor. In addition, he was probably scared of Hispanic leaders ready to cry racism if Republicans advocated following the existing law, building the border fence and prosecuting businesses that knowingly hire illegal labor.

We may never know all of his fears, but we do know that while the GOP was frozen with inaction, the president aggressively moved forward with his radical agenda. Such timidity only helped "outsider" presidential candidates like Donald Trump in 2016.

The cowardly GOP Congressional response enraged many conservatives and Independents who voted for the GOP in the mid-term elections. They have seen no action from Congress on executive amnesty and other issues, so many have left the GOP while others may give the party one more chance: the 2016 election.

For the remainder of his time as Speaker, John Boehner delivered nothing but stale rhetoric. He was a lousy Speaker of the House, and the perfect recipient of "Turkey of the Year" award.

The Controversial Bush Legacy

The real race for the GOP nomination began on December 16, 2014, when former Florida Governor Jeb Bush announced that he would "actively explore" the presidency. Thus, the 23-month marathon to the next presidential election officially started.

In every GOP nomination battle there are two main sides: the establishment versus the conservatives. There was no better representative of the establishment than a member of the Bush family. The conservative side is more varied; in 2016 it has been represented by a large list of candidates, including Governors, Senators and wild cards.

The 2016 nomination battle is proving to be particularly fierce and "wide open," as predicted by former House Speaker Newt Gingrich. In his view, the race will be heavily contested and the most "open on our side since 1940." Gingrich is an expert on the topic, since he lost the 2012 GOP nomination contest to moderate heartthrob Mitt Romney.

While moderates have so often been successful in winning the nomination, the record shows that since 1992, they have either lost the White House or, in the case of George W. Bush, won while masquerading as a conservative.

In the current election, a conservative presidential nominee will give the Republicans the best chance of defeating a liberal Democrat opponent. Unfortunately, now as always, the challenge is to wrest the nomination away from the party's moderate establishment wing, which always has superior funding and political endorsements.

Another critical problem for conservatives is that their votes are usually split between several viable presidential candidates. In the 2012 contest, Mitt Romney was the only moderate candidate in the race and garnered universal support from that wing of the party. In contrast, his conservative opponents were not able to consolidate support or funding in time to battle Romney throughout the long nomination process.

In this contest Bush was initially a favorite, but faced competition from other moderate candidates. The conservative side started with no apparent frontrunner, but included several big names such as businessman Donald Trump, Texas Senator Ted Cruz, Wisconsin Governor Scott Walker and pediatric neurosurgeon Dr. Ben Carson.

By December of 2014, the clock was ticking for the candidates, and there was not as much time as usual. The Republican Party set the convention for July 18-21, 2016, much earlier than normal. In the space of half a year the serious contenders would have to get noticed, make the top ten to qualify for the presidential debates, and raise enough money to wage an expensive battle on the airwaves. The race started with at least 17 well known GOP contenders, but, eventually, only a few such as Trump and Cruz became legitimate candidates for the nomination.

Several conservatives struggled for funding, but that was never a problem for Jeb Bush. He enjoyed plenty of big money donations and PAC support. His last name gave him a tremendous advantage with the insiders. Nonetheless, it eventually became a handicap as millions of conservatives expressed their distaste for the Bush family continuing to control the Republican Party.

The legacy of the Bush family was a big negative for Jeb, as both his brother and father were in many respects failed Presidents. Like them, Jeb also advocates positions that anger true conservatives. For example, he supports the controversial Common Core educational program; he supports immigration reform, which conservatives believe is glorified amnesty; he is an advocate of gun purchase background checks; and he is not a supporter of the National Rifle Association.

Among many reputable conservatives, Bush's record is very troubling. Overall, he is "a very good moderate Democrat," according to talk show host Mark Levin. Legendary conservative activist Richard Viguerie says that conservatives "don't trust" Jeb Bush. In the view of Regan biographer Craig Shirley, the Bush family has a very troubling history of battling conservatives as they "got their start in 1980 opposing Reagan and Reaganism, as they continue to do today."

In making his Facebook announcement, Bush declared that he wanted to restore the "promise of America." In reality, he wanted to return ultimate political power to his family and continue the Bush dynasty. Our country's promise cannot be restored by electing the third member of the Bush family since 1993 to serve as president.

As Donald Trump noted, our country "does not need another Bush." Thankfully, the Founding Fathers created a Constitutional republic, not a monarchy.

VIII

2015
GOP re-elects Boehner, Tells Conservatives to "Go to Hell"

Despite his lame track record of backing down to Obama and his repeated betrayal of conservatives, John Boehner was re-elected as Speaker of the House on January 6, 2015. Boehner was re-elected despite the news uncovered by Dr. Jerome Corsi that the Speaker had a stock portfolio that included millions of dollars invested in insurance and healthcare companies, which increased in value due to Obamacare. Thus, he had a financial incentive to disregard the party's base and continue to implement the president's plans for socialized medicine.

By re-electing Boehner, Republican Party leaders in the House essentially told conservatives to "go to hell." It was another indication that the party was not the right home for principled conservatives. Nothing else explains the incomprehensible vote to re-elect John Boehner as Speaker of the House.

Boehner was a disaster as Speaker. During his tenure, conservatives were punished and denied leadership positions, while the establishment wing of the GOP was given total control. Under Boehner, spending accelerated and real reform was minimal. Boehner was the president's golfing buddy, not the type of leader who strenuously opposed him. While the American people wanted the Republicans to stop the president's dangerously liberal agenda, the House Republicans under Boehner constantly placated him.

This betrayal enraged conservatives who bombarded Congress with demands that Republicans select a new Speaker of the House. Phone calls overwhelmed the Congressional switchboard, while millions of emails were sent to Republican members of Congress telling them to listen to the people and not the Beltway power brokers. The conservative website WorldNetDaily organized a "Dump Boehner" campaign that resulted in almost 600,000 letters being sent to Congress.

Instead, the members of the GOP Congressional delegation re-elected Boehner to a third term. While there were a historic number of votes against Boehner in his bid for a third term as Speaker, it was not enough to stop his re-election. The vote showed that once again conservatives had been taken for granted.

After Boehner's re-election, conservatives had every right to reexamine their allegiance to the Republican Party. Republicans always campaign as conservatives yet govern like liberals. Was this another case of business as usual on Capitol Hill? Fortunately, the outrage continued to grow throughout 2015. Life became very difficult for Boehner as the grassroots pressure never abated and conservative members of Congress started to oppose him more and more often. After being threatened with a potential vote of no confidence and the prospect of actually being ousted, Boehner eventually had no other option but to resign from his position as Speaker. Conservatives won a key victory when Boehner was forced from his position and resigned on September 26, 2015.

This victory was an anomaly for conservatives, who mostly suffered losses in Congress. In contrast, there was a building enthusiasm for the presidential race of 2016 as more and more conservatives were energized about their chances of electing one of their own in 2016. The key will be for the GOP to nominate a conservative as the standard bearer. Otherwise, Hillary Clinton, or whoever becomes the Democratic Party nominates, can start measuring the curtains in the White House.

The Formula for GOP Victory in 2016

After two long terms of Barack Obama, the country should be ready for a change in 2016. This president delivered a constant dose of no-compromise liberalism that divided the races and polarized the political climate.

Given a grand opportunity to seize the White House, the GOP launched its presidential campaign earlier than ever. But that's not enough. Only a conservative president in the White House can undo Obama's disastrous policies.

First comes winning the nomination and then the general election—no easy task for Republicans. Barack Obama, despite having limited experience and a very liberal philosophy, was elected president in 2008 and retained the office four years later, even though his signature legislation, the Affordable Care Act, was incredibly unpopular.

One of the major reasons for his success was his unimpressive opposition. The Republican presidential nominees in those two elections, John McCain in 2008 and Mitt Romney in 2012, were uninspiring moderates who were unwilling to aggressively defend the party's platform and attack the Democrats on the issues. Given the horrific track record of establishment Republicans since 1996, it would seem that party honchos would be desperate to find a good conservative to win the presidential nomination in 2016. On the contrary, GOP party bosses were giddy, at least initially, about the candidacy of Jeb Bush, and were also willing to support New Jersey Governor Chris Christie, South Carolina Senator Lindsey Graham, Ohio Governor John Kasich, and former New York Governor George Pataki as back-ups if necessary. This was an embarrassment of riches for the party's elites, who usually have only one presidential candidate to support in a particular election year.

Sadly, these same elites always seem to be more concerned about winning the nomination than winning the general election. As history has shown, moderate Republican candidates lose presidential elections. The exceptions to this rule are the 1988 victory of George H. W. Bush, which was in essence the third term of the very popular President Ronald Reagan, and the 2004 election of George W. Bush, in the aftermath of 9/11 and the surge of patriotism as the country was at war. Remember that in the 2000 election, Bush won the race, but lost the popular vote.

There's a simple reason for such predictable results: A moderate presidential candidate does not excite the conservative base of Republican voters. Thus, they do not turn out to vote in big numbers, which is what happened to Romney in 2012. Conservatives are the backbone of the Republican Party. Most of the Party's chronic voters, activists, volunteers and organizational leaders are conservatives.

Many of these activists have been waiting since Ronald Reagan for a conservative nominee. They are tired of being overlooked and ignored by the establishment wing of the Republican Party. Grassroots conservatives cannot match the money available to the establishment, but they certainly have more passion and energy and are a needed component for any GOP presidential candidate to win the White House.

This formula worked for Ronald Reagan in 1980 and 1984. He won 44 states in the first election and 49 states in his re-election—in other words, massive landslides. According to so-called political experts he was too conservative, a wild eyed cowboy who was too threatening to the American people.

But instead of losing, he trounced his liberal opponents by offering a clear contrast to the Democratic Party. He stood on conservative principles and did not waver. This type of statesmanship appealed to not only Republicans, but also Independents and "Reagan Democrats," who were tired of the failed liberal policies of their party.

The 2016 election provides a great opportunity for the Republican Party. Voters are ready to seriously consider an alternative to the failed policies of Obama. However, if the GOP offers only the "pale pastels" of another moderate loser and not the "bold colors" of a conservative, the party will surely lose again.

If Bush or another moderate wins the nomination, millions of conservatives will stay away from the polls or vote third party. The days of holding one's nose and voting for the Republican candidate as the "lesser of two evils" are over.

It is time for a conservative victory in 2016, but this will require a principled Republican Party presidential nominee. If an establishment candidate prevails again, the result will be another loss to the Democrats and the eventual dissolution of the Grand Old Party. Conservatives will tire of being used and abused by an elite party structure that has no interest in listening to their demands, only forcing them to accept nominees acceptable to the establishment.

In GOP Race, It's as Easy as ABC: Anybody but Bush or Christie

By February of 2015, with 21 months until the November 2016 presidential election, it was clear to everyone that the GOP field of candidates would be large and impressive. At that point, approximately two dozen prominent Republicans had expressed an interest in running for president. Of course, not all of them would actually run, but it was encouraging that most of the candidates were strong conservatives with solid credentials.

Unfortunately, the field also included two well-known moderates: former Florida Governor Jeb Bush and New Jersey Governor Chris Christie, both of whom were able to raise large sums of money and become major factors in the upcoming election.

The most serious establishment candidate was former Florida Governor Jeb Bush, who was initially the odds-on favorite to secure the presidential nomination. Bush, with his strong name recognition, led in all the early polls. He was supposedly going to be difficult to beat.

In the early part of the campaign, Bush aggressively worked to lock up big donors and key activists. His campaign organization was so strong it forced Mitt Romney to exit the race before he officially entered it. In early January of 2015, Romney had announced to a small gathering of donors that he was interested in running for president a third time. However, when he started trying to build a campaign network across the country, he realized that Jeb Bush had already signed up many of the top GOP contributors and consultants. Romney came to the realization that he could not raise enough money to seriously challenge Bush for the nomination, so, three weeks after floating a trial balloon expressing interest, he officially decided not to run for president.

With Romney out, Bush's chances were even better. Unfortunately, he was plain wrong on an array of issues such as taxes, immigration and Common Core. He even made the ludicrous comment that Romney lost in 2012 because he ran too far to the right.

Those moderates who were not enamored with Bush had a viable alternative: New Jersey Governor Chris Christie. He was a moderate on social issues, such as gay marriage, and immigration; he had supported the DREAM Act. In addition he was an advocate of stricter gun laws, which might have been popular in New Jersey but was viewed much differently in the South. Overall, like Bush, Christie was just wrong on too many issues.

It should have been easy to predict that both candidates would eventually fail; however, as discussed, the moderate wing or establishment of the party had assumed total control of the GOP nomination process after the Reagan years. This wing is usually at odds with the more conservative or grassroots activists of the party, often associated with the Tea Party movement. Most moderates view Tea Party activists with disdain and are working tirelessly to prevent a conservative from achieving the nomination in 2016.

Conservatism works as a framework for both governing and winning elections. Hopefully, a majority of Republican Party voters will come to this realization in time to save their party and, more importantly, their country.

Dear Barbara Bush

Dear Barbara Bush,
Thank you so much for your thoughtful March 20, 2015 "friend" letter that you sent me and millions of other Americans. You were so kind to solicit donations on behalf of your son Jeb's presidential

campaign. Of course, you let us know that you "changed your mind" because on April 25, 2013 you told Matt Lauer of the "Today" show that "there are other people out there that are very qualified and we've had enough Bushes."

I realize that it is a woman's prerogative to change her mind. I also am not surprised that you now have a different view regarding Jeb's aspirations and want to support him since he is surely running for president. Nonetheless, I must respectfully decline your request and inform you that I will be encouraging everyone I know to emphatically tell you "no" as well.

I do not hate the Bush family, for I know all of you are patriotic Americans. However, I must note that the Bush family has done tremendous harm to this nation. Your husband was elected president because of Ronald Reagan, yet squandered his legacy. George H. W. Bush broke his promise to the American people and raised taxes, thus giving the nation the plague of Bill and Hillary Clinton.

Your son was even worse. George W. inherited a large budget surplus, but created expensive entitlements, a massive new government department and pursued out of control domestic spending and unfunded foreign wars. He turned the surplus into a $468 billion deficit for his successor, and left the country an additional $5 trillion in debt.

Your son Jeb is a nice guy, but he is as uncharismatic as your husband and other son, George W. More importantly, he is wrong on too many important issues. He is pro-amnesty, will not rule out higher taxes, supports Common Core, and believes the moderate Mitt Romney ran a presidential campaign that was too far to the right.

On foreign policy, it has been revealed that one of Jeb's advisers is former Secretary of State James Baker, a creature of the Beltway who is infamous for his anti-Israeli views. Baker is a well-known

GOP insider and moderate who supports establishment candidates and loathes Tea Party activists. For icing on the proverbial cake, it was just reported that Jeb is friends with a fugitive who is evading justice in Spain. Clearly, he has the wrong type of friends.

Speaking of friends, in your letter, Mrs. Bush, you wrote, "We need and appreciate your help, friend. Thank you for your support and I look forward to counting you among our ranks." You may call me "friend," but don't count on my support. As a "friend," let me remind you of your statement to Matt Lauer less than two years ago, "there are a lot of great families and it's not just four families.... he'll (Jeb) get all our enemies, half our friends."

Well, I am in the group of "friends" who are not with Jeb. Here is the most important reason why I do not support him: he will lose. If Jeb runs, the Republican ticket will surely lose and our country will be subjected to four years of Hillary Clinton or whatever crazed liberal is nominated by the Democratic Party. Our country cannot afford four more years of a liberal in the White House. We need a conservative, the only type of Republican nominee who can win. Sadly, your son, like the entire Bush family, is *not* a conservative.

Mrs. Bush, while you may have changed your mind about Jeb running, I have not. What you said less than two years ago is still true today; our country has had "enough Bushes."

Sincerely, Jeff Crouere

Republicans Lose Faith in Party Leadership

A May 22, 2015 Pew Research poll showed that the country was very unhappy with the GOP-led Congress. In fact, Americans were so disgusted that Republican Congressional leaders registered only a 22% overall approval rating.

What was especially significant was that this anger is bipartisan. Only 41% of Republicans approved of the performance of the GOP Congressional leadership, much lower than the 60% approval rating GOP leaders received in 2011 and the astounding 78% approval rating they received from Republicans in 1995, months after the party took control of Congress for the first time in 40 years.

There is a major difference between the Congressional leadership of today and the team that led Congress in 1995. During that era, Newt Gingrich was Speaker of the House. In the November 1994 elections, Americans sent Congressional Republicans to Capitol Hill with a mission: enact the Contract with America. Led by Gingrich, Congress was actually able to get some tangible goals accomplished by moving then-president Bill Clinton to the right. As a result, Clinton signed into law bills that lowered capital gains taxes and established welfare reform. Even more miraculous, a significant budget surplus was created.

Gingrich was an unabashed movement conservative who truly believed in the concepts of lower taxes and less government. Unfortunately, today, the GOP leadership in Congress are typical establishment Republicans who have been on Capitol Hill too long. They are opposed to the Tea Party and true conservatives, and thus they have no interest in real reform or following the wishes of the vast majority of grassroots Republicans throughout the country.

A mere four months after the Republicans officially took control of the Senate and House, the strong majority of the GOP electorate had already lost faith in the Congressional leadership. Who could blame them, since almost nothing was accomplished? Congress did pass the Keystone Pipeline bill, only to see it vetoed by President Obama; and the House did pass a bill ending abortions after the 20th week of pregnancy. But on almost everything else there was no legislative action, only rhetoric.

Despite the fact that almost every Republican Congressional candidate campaigned against Obamacare and the president's unconstitutional executive amnesty for five million illegal aliens, Congress voted to fund both programs. The Senate approved the radical nomination of Loretta Lynch as the new Attorney General and gave Obama a major victory by approving legislation giving him more power to enact trade deals.

The trade promotion authority will force Congress in 2016 to accept the upcoming Trans-Pacific Partnership deal between the United States and 11 other nations without adding any amendments. It will force Congress to make an up or down vote on the trade pact, in effect making it "fast track" legislation. This legislation is viewed by some analysts as another gift to big business at the expense of the jobs of middle income and hard-working Americans, and many conservatives are upset that Congress approved legislation that gives the president more power. However, both Boehner and McConnell were very supportive of the Trans-Pacific Partnership

The Republicans in Congress did a pitiful job of advancing any type of conservative agenda or standing up to President Obama. This betrayal of the grassroots in their own party was clearly reflected in the Pew poll. The stage is set for the 2016 presidential race, where true conservative candidates are facing establishment-supported candidates. The results have been encouraging since the candidate with the most connections and support among party leaders, former Florida Governor Jeb Bush, failed miserably.

The More the Merrier in GOP Presidential Race

The first week of June, 2015 was a very busy one in the GOP presidential sweepstakes. Two more candidates jumped into the race: U.S. Senator Lindsey Graham of South Carolina and former Texas Governor Rick Perry. Soon, an incredible 17 presidential candidates had entered the fray. The candidates were grouped in several different ways. For example, former Arkansas Governor Mike Huckabee and former Pennsylvania Senator Rick Santorum emphasized social issues, while former Texas Governor Rick Perry and U.S. Senator Lindsey Graham (R-SC) focused on national security, and U.S. Senator Rand Paul of Kentucky concentrated on protecting the liberties Americans are guaranteed by the Bill of Rights. However, there was another way to group the candidates: "conservative" or "RINO." Clearly, former Florida Governor Jeb Bush was the best funded and leading RINO, but it was still not clear who would assume the mantle as the top conservative contender.

Due to the plethora of conservative candidates, some commentators lamented our embarrassment of riches. They called for conservatives to unite behind one candidate who could defeat Bush. However, it was far too early for any consolidation among the candidates. Voters needed to see the candidates in action, witness them in a debate setting and learn where they stand on the major issues. In essence, the Republican race became an example of a political free market, as voters were given a wide variety of choices from which to choose the best candidate.

Such a decision should rest with the voters, not kingmakers or journalists. Sadly, news networks like Fox and CNN exercised plenty of power by limiting the initial presidential debates to only the "top ten" candidates. It was not college football, but the future of the nation that was being determined, so limiting the field of candidates was premature and adversely impacted the decision making ability of voters.

The networks were supposedly going to decide the "top ten" based on an average of early polls, but they were too influenced by name recognition alone. A larger debate format would have been an essential public service, especially with the future of our nation at risk. The 2016 election will be the most important one in our lifetime, as the next president must repair the damage done by Barack Obama to our nation's economy, national security and social fabric, namely race relations.

In 2016, the stakes are high and the country is in serious trouble. From the beginning the presidential race featured the largest field of viable candidates ever presented to Republican voters. This plethora of choices has been very positive and it is in stark contrast to the very limited field offered to Democrat voters.

From an initial group of 17 candidates, the field has narrowed significantly. Yet, as voters make their final decision, it is essential, especially in this troubled environment, that GOP voters nominate a conservative. In this way, Republican voters will have the very best chance to defeat Hillary Clinton and spare the nation a third Obama administration.

Trump Towers Over GOP Field

On June 16, 2015, the GOP race for president took a very different turn as real estate billionaire Donald Trump entered the fray. After three decades of flirting with the idea of running for president, Trump finally made the official plunge in front of a crowd of supporters at Trump Tower in New York City. With his entrance, there were 12 announced candidates contending for the GOP nomination.

In his speech, Trump vowed to "make America great again." He said he will focus on creating jobs and noted that the official unemployment rate is far lower than the reality. While the administration touts an official rate of under 5%, Trump believes the true rate is closer to 25% or more.

During his lengthy remarks, Trump skewered the president's handling of the war against ISIS; our trade policies with China; and our country's lax immigration policies, among many other issues. He promised to build a fence on the Southern border and "have Mexico pay for that wall, mark my words." He also pledged to rebuild the military, take a tough stance with Iran and repeal the "disaster" of Obamacare.

The essence of Trump's speech was that he would restore the American Dream. With the elegant backdrop of the Trump Tower behind him, the Donald was showcasing to the American people his accomplishments and promising to achieve greatness for his country as well.

Although the political elite completely dismissed Trump's chance to win the White House, in reality there were a number of reasons why he should never have been overlooked. First, he has achieved incredible success in his professional life. Trump built a real estate empire and established a number of very successful businesses, employing thousands of people. Along with his success in the business world, he created a very popular television show, *The Apprentice*. This reality TV franchise was on the air for 14 seasons, with Trump as the star—no small achievement.

With a net worth of over $10 billion, Trump was like no other candidate in the race, easily able to self-finance a serious nationwide campaign for the nomination. Unlike his opponents, Trump did not have to spend any time raising money. He focused all his energies on campaigning and earning the votes of the GOP electorate.

After his announcement he spent a few days making numerous media appearances as well as campaign stops in Iowa and New Hampshire. While Trump had never been an official candidate prior to this year, he had accumulated years of experience doing public speaking events and television interviews. This was one candidate who did not need any media training.

Over the next few months, Trump did not deviate from the message he had outlined in his announcement speech. On the campaign trail he was able to easily motivate conservative audiences by emphasizing the signature issues he discussed at his launch.

In business and in the media, Trump has enjoyed massive success. It remains to be seen whether this will translate into the ultimate victory in the political world, but at least he does not have to worry about building name recognition among the public due to his decades in the public eye.

Trump enjoys another significant advantage over some of his rather youthful opponents in the race: he has years of business and negotiation experience, both nationally and internationally. At the age of 69, Donald Trump is a household name. He spent a career building wealth and his brand, and entered the presidential race in a major way despite having to build political support for the first time. Based on his business track record, his positions on the issues and his incredible resources, it would be very unwise to discount the Donald's chances.

Trump vs. Political Correctness

When Donald Trump announced for president, he made some strong statements about the immigration problems facing our nation. He said that Mexico was "bringing drugs, they're bringing crime, they're rapists, and some, I assume, are good people." In essence, Trump noted that Mexico was not sending its scientists and scholars to America.

In this speech he mentioned that while immigrants are taking jobs in this country, corporations like Ford are setting up plants in Mexico. To deal with the crisis, Trump vowed to build a border fence and have Mexico pay for it.

This kind of tough talk resonated with millions of Americans who have seen no action on the border for decades. In the first New Hampshire GOP poll after his announcement, Trump rocketed to second place behind only Jeb Bush. This showed that Americans were tired of the influx of illegal immigrants, and nonexistent border security. Of course, illegal aliens do commit crimes, receive federal benefits and take jobs away from law-abiding citizens.

It is an outrage that our borders are still not secure after decades of promises. In fact, no other nation in the world has such wide open borders with such generous benefits for illegal aliens. Donald Trump wants this giveaway of American jobs and federal incentives to end. He wants to secure our border and improve our national security. These are goals that all Americans should applaud; however, in our politically correct society, such goals are too controversial.

In the aftermath of his announcement, NBC "fired" Trump from his show *Celebrity Apprentice* and said they would not air the Miss USA or Miss Universe pageants that they co-own with the Donald. Trump's illegal immigration comments were also too controversial for Univision, which also dropped the beauty pageants from their broadcast schedule. Thus, the pageants were left without a broadcast network, and *Celebrity Apprentice* proceeded with Arnold Schwarzenegger as the new star host.

Sadly, both networks succumbed to the pressure of Hispanic groups and the ever-present specter of political correctness. Clearly, Trump had not lied about the border problems, but these networks and the politicians in Washington, who are funded by special interests, do not want to deal with the problem. Democrats benefit from the cheap votes, and the big business supporters of the GOP benefit from the cheap labor. The casualties of the open border policy are those Americans who lose their jobs or become victims of the criminal activity of illegal aliens.

The good news is that Trump is not like all the other politicians who would have apologized or backtracked from controversial comments. Instead, he doubled down and fired back at NBC and Univision, threatening to sue them. In a priceless statement, Trump blasted NBC as the network that "will stand behind lying Brian Williams, but won't stand behind people who tell it like it is, as unpleasant as that may be."

How true. America today is filled with people who are afraid to "tell it like it is." Fortunately, one of these truth-tellers is running for president. Let's see if the American people want the truth or if they prefer to maintain their belief in fiction supported only by politically correct lies.

As Trump's campaign has progressed, he stands firm with his message and continues to find support from Americans who have been ignored for decades. Today, our problems are so severe it is time for not only tough talk, but, more importantly, strong action. Political correctness has done incredible damage. It is a very serious affliction on this country that will eventually destroy America if it is not pulled up by the roots and eradicated.

GOP Elite: A Confederacy of Dunces

Members of the GOP establishment have been beyond upset by these developments: they have been apoplectic. On the day their favored candidate, former Florida Governor Jeb Bush, announced for president, he was immediately overshadowed by Donald Trump, who officially entered the race the next day.

Ever since then it has been all Trump, all the time. From his bold statements to his refusal to apologize, he has dominated media coverage. Americans did not even know what Mr. Moderate, Jeb Bush, was doing anymore. First, Trump got blasted by Hispanic groups and business leaders for his comments about illegal immigration; next, he was pilloried by the RNC and Republican politicians for his remarks that, in essence, U.S. Senator John McCain was a war hero "because he was captured" by the enemy.

Before the McCain firestorm died down, Trump created a new controversy by releasing the cell phone number of U.S. Senator Lindsey Graham (R-SC) in retaliation for Graham calling Trump a "jackass," even though several years earlier the Senator had begged Trump to help him get on Fox News.

The week ended with Trump telling Anderson Cooper of CNN that the public doesn't trust the media, and then visiting the border and bringing attention to his favorite issue. Through it all, he was several steps ahead of his multitude of opponents, and creating a bond with conservative voters who have been looking for a champion.

Since Reagan, conservatives have been searching for a candidate who will not apologize, nor let the media and the captains of political correctness dictate the debate. Simultaneously, Trump went to war with the GOP establishment, the media, old guard Republican politicians and his fellow presidential candidates such as former Texas Governor Rick Perry. Perry called Trump a "cancer" on conservatism, while Trump basically called Perry an imbecile who tried to look smarter by wearing glasses. With the exception of U.S. Senator Ted Cruz, all the other candidates—called "midgets" by conservative commentator Ann Coulter—joined in the Trump bashing, and lost conservative support as a result.

Every day there was a new attack against Trump, who always returned fire and loved every minute of it. He also attacked the smug "conservative" pundits like George Will and Charles Krauthammer, who were appalled at him and his campaign. While the battles continued, Trump surged in the polls and started to enjoy a double-digit lead over Bush, his nearest GOP challenger.

Why did Trump take the lead? Because he criticized all of the groups that conservatives hate: the media, Republican moderates, and the party establishment. Millions of conservatives know that the GOP has been taken over by the country club wing, and are ready to bolt the Republican Party if this trend continued.

Sadly, the elite refused to receive this loud and clear message. At the Republican Governor's Conference, party bigwigs conspired to keep Trump out of the presidential debates, even though he was leading in the polls! If that failed, they hoped to convince other candidates such as Bush and Wisconsin Governor Scott Walker to boycott the debates if Trump participated. Eventually, the harebrained plan was rejected, but only after it had been leaked to the media.

This showed once again how afraid the GOP establishment was of Trump. He is so wealthy that he does not need their money. He has established name recognition due to decades of business and media activities. If the idiots who run the GOP continue to insult Trump and block his path to the nomination, they are almost guaranteeing that he will run as an Independent in the presidential race.

If that happens, many conservatives will vote for Trump over any moderate GOP nominee, a Democrat lite like Jeb Bush. If Trump does opt for a presidential run as an Independent, he will do better than Ross Perot did in 1992 and 1996. He might not win, but he will impact the race.

It is up to "geniuses" who control the Republican Party: Do they just want to keep control of the party, or do they actually want to win the general election?

Trump's Nuclear Option

From the very beginning of the first GOP presidential debate in August, Donald Trump was in the spotlight and under fire from Fox News commentators. The first question asked for a show of hands of all candidates who would not pledge to support whoever the Republican presidential nominee turned out to be. Only Donald Trump raised his hand, which led to the first of many confrontations during the debate. He was challenged by debate moderator Brett Baier and lambasted by Senator Rand Paul for "buying and selling politicians." While Trump declared that he wanted to "run as the Republican nominee," he was absolutely correct to keep his options open.

Throughout the campaign, the Republican establishment has been terrified of Trump and his independence from special interests. They know that he can easily finance a third party campaign for the presidency. This was exactly why Trump kept the third party option open: it maintained his "leverage." This decision might provide a needed option for the American people in November 2016, especially if the presidential nominees are Hillary Clinton versus an establishment Republican.

Although Trump eventually signed a pledge and promised to support the GOP nominee, he said that he would be loyal only if he was treated fairly by the party. If Trump is unfairly denied the GOP nomination, he could still run as an Independent candidate. At least it would give voters a real alternative. The last thing the country needs is another Bush or Clinton in the White House.

In fact, in a three-way race between Hillary Clinton, an establishment Republican like John Kasich for example and Donald Trump, there is at least a possibility that Trump might win. There is great dissatisfaction with political dynasties, and millions of Americans would refuse to vote for either Clinton or Bush, giving a well-funded third party candidate like Trump a chance.

There is certainly precedent for a strong third party candidacy. Back in 1992, businessman Ross Perot was leading the presidential race before he exited amid claims that he did not want to throw the race into the House of Representatives. He later said he was really concerned that Republicans were planning to disrupt his daughter's wedding, so he had to get out of the race. When he returned to the campaign months later, his prospects were severely diminished. Nevertheless, he finished with approximately 19% of the vote, the highest third party total since Theodore Roosevelt in 1912.

Unlike Perot, who destroyed his chances when he left the race, Trump would be a more serious third party contender if he chose to enter the race in that role. He has universal name recognition, billions of dollars at his disposal, and no need to placate special interests or big money donors. Clearly, the GOP establishment, and their supporters in the media, will try to destroy his chances. This is exactly what happened during the first Fox News debate.

Trump spent the debate fending off questions about his bankruptcies, his treatment of women, and his previous support of Democrat candidates. Throughout it all, Trump stayed on the offensive and refused to apologize. This stance was popular with the vast conservative audience of the Drudge Report website. After 531,000 votes were tabulated, Trump was declared the debate winner by over 45% of the voters, way ahead of second-place finisher Ted Cruz, who received 14% of the vote. While the public loved Trump's performance, so-called experts such as analyst Charles Krauthammer and pollster Frank Luntz panned The Donald's showing. In true Trump fashion, he blasted Luntz as a "low class slob."

Clearly, Trump's best chance for victory would be as the GOP nominee. Obviously, he would prefer to win the Republican nomination; however, he might be subjected to impossible hurdles as the race progresses. At this point, the race is still ongoing, so it is too early to determine what will happen, but we do know that since Donald Trump is involved, everyone will be watching.

Trump vs. the Foolish & Phony Experts

When Donald Trump burst on the political scene as a presidential candidate in June of 2015, commentators and pollsters who populate cable news programs—the so-called "experts"—claimed it was all a publicity stunt. Then they said he would never release his financial statements. Then they said his controversial comments about immigration, Senator John McCain and Fox News Host Megyn Kelly would doom his campaign.

Eventually, they bellowed that his lead was temporary and would soon reach a "ceiling." In essence, they called his campaign a flash in the pan. Unfortunately for the "experts," they were wrong on every one of their talking points. Trump started to solidify his lead, even though the liberal media and the Republican establishment wished it would disappear. He upset their meticulous plan for the GOP to nominate another moderate candidate such as Jeb Bush, and once again lose to the Democrats.

Fortunately, Trump did not follow their losing script. He is used to winning in business and in the media, and expects to win the presidential race. His confidence was infectious and encouraged more support among Republican voters. Soon the majority of Republicans expressed the belief that Trump would win the nomination.

A late August 2015 Rasmussen poll showed that 57% of GOP voters believed Trump would be the next Republican presidential nominee. During that same period, a Fox News poll showed Trump with a double-digit lead (25-12%) over his nearest competitor, Jeb Bush. In a match-up versus Hillary Clinton, the same Fox News poll had Trump gaining significant ground, only trailing 52-47% while the CNN national poll had Trump trailing Clinton by a 51-45% margin, closer than other Republican candidates such as businesswoman Carly Fiorina, Wisconsin Governor Scott Walker, or Jeb Bush.

These results actually showed that Trump was the most electable candidate. However, a succession of Fox News analysts such as columnist George Will, commentator Charles Krauthammer and consultant Karl Rove criticized Trump as either a clown or someone who was too bombastic to be taken seriously. They stated that his tactics and message were actually harmful to the Republican Party, and that other candidates were more electable. Once again, it seemed the so-called "experts" were wrong and, in fact, the real clowns are the commentators who have been on television too long and live in the Washington D.C. bubble.

They were also not objective. George Will's wife worked as a consultant for Governor Walker, and Rove was obviously for Jeb Bush. Rove has a long history with the Bush family, and served in the White House during the administration of George W. Bush.

These analysts were given screen time because Fox News and most other media outlets were opposed to Trump and his conservative message. In reality, they tried to destroy Trump. For evidence, just look at the Fox News GOP presidential debate. Nonetheless, the liberal media continue to cover Trump because he is interesting. He is a colorful, combative candidate, while his opponents are mostly boring and uninteresting.

As Trump noted, Bush is a "low energy" candidate while The Donald has plenty of energy, enthusiasm and passion for this country. His campaign slogan said it all: "Make America Great Again." Unlike Hillary, who avoids the media and runs from their questions, Trump is constantly doing interviews, conducting long news conferences and hosting raucous and entertaining town hall meetings.

The biggest crowd of the early campaign showed up on August 21, 2015 in Mobile, Alabama, where Trump delivered a speech to over 30,000 people. Without doubt, it was a bigger crowd than anything that Bush, Clinton or any other candidate could attract. At that point, even the skeptical news media and GOP insiders had to admit that the Trump Train was heading down the track with its sights set on the White House.

Time for RNC to Finally Show Loyalty to Conservatives

When Trump finally acquiesced and signed the loyalty pledge, it was a victory for the RNC, which had been pressuring him for weeks. The document was signed with much fanfare at the Trump Tower in New York City in front of RNC Chairman Reince Preibus.

The "loyalty" issue had been extremely important to GOP leadership. Party leaders were terrified that Trump would run as a third party candidate in the 2016 election and doom their chances of victory. Until signing the pledge, Trump maintained his interest in exploring a third party bid if the RNC treated him poorly. He said that it gave him "leverage" in the upcoming race. Obviously, at that point, Trump decided that he would win the GOP nomination and no longer needed the leverage. The late summer polls showed Trump at 30% support, with a double digit lead over second place challenger, Dr. Ben Carson, who had replaced Jeb Bush in that position.

Now that Trump had signed this pledge, it was time for the RNC to finally show some loyalty to the base of their party, the conservatives. It is quite ironic that a group that has been incredibly unfaithful and disloyal to conservatives would demand a loyalty pledge from the leading candidate. Donald Trump should not have been forced to sign any sort of ridiculous pledge. It was reminiscent of the Communist Party tactic of forcing members to support the leadership or face the consequences.

Trump's decision means that conservatives might once again be left out in the cold come November 2016. If the Republicans nominate a moderate candidate and the Democrats nominate a typical liberal like Hillary Clinton, conservatives will be faced with their familiar paradox: choosing the lesser of two evils.

Conservatives have been loyal to the RNC for too long. The party establishment no longer deserves the loyalty of either candidates or voters. In this election, conservatives should vote for the Republican nominee only if the candidate espouses their values and shares their positions on important issues. The era of holding your nose and voting Republican needs to end, otherwise it will be another frustrating presidential election season.

Let's hope that Donald Trump or another conservative wins the Republican presidential nomination in 2016 and can start to demolish the destructive GOP establishment. If not, it is time that conservatives find another party more deserving of their loyalty.

Trump Exposed Fox News Bias against Conservatives

Ever since it was launched in 1996, Fox News has enjoyed an ever-growing television audience. Talk show host Rush Limbaugh often promoted Fox News in the early years of the network, helping to establish the connection with conservatives across the country. In fact, thanks to Rush and others on talk radio, Fox News has enjoyed tremendous ratings growth over the last 20 years.

Today, Fox News is the unquestioned ratings champion among cable news channels. One other factor determining ratings success has been the unpopularity of the hard left content being delivered by competitors such as CNN and MSNBC. Viewers interested in coverage that was not titled to the hard left had nowhere to turn but Fox News.

On the other hand, while it is not a liberal network, Fox News is not friendly to true conservatives either. Most Fox News hosts are either moderate or downright liberal. The midday host, Shephard

Smith, is blatantly liberal on a wide variety of issues. For example, he blasted conservatives who supported border security and limiting Muslim immigration, and criticized those who mentioned the liberalism of Pope Francis.

Evening hosts such as Greta Van Susteren and Bill O'Reilly are Independents who are fairly moderate on most issues. Megyn Kelly has some conservative views, but her efforts to derail Donald Trump were easily apparent to the viewers of her program. While Sean Hannity is a conservative, his favorite guests are typically members of the Republican establishment, who often battle conservatives on endorsements and policies.

The network consistently uses analysts who routinely criticize Trump. Supposed experts such as George Will, Charles Krauthammer, Brit Hume and Karl Rove are card-carrying members of the GOP establishment who see Trump as a threat. Not surprisingly, these Fox News guests and so-called experts regularly attack Trump, yet the network rarely balances those views with guests representing the Tea Party or other conservative groups.

By late September, the attacks might have played a role in some poll slippage for Trump. Nevertheless, he still led the GOP race for the nomination, with his strongest base of support represented by Tea Party conservatives. But instead of championing Trump's level of support, Fox News focused on issues and guests who were critical of the front runner. In fact, Trump spokesman Michael Cohen claimed that Fox News was "marginalizing him" and "criticizing him," and "trying to figure out how to get this man out of the race."

From the moment he entered the race, Trump began expressing concern about the type of media coverage he was receiving. During the first debate, Fox News targeted Trump with a variety of hostile questions, with Kelly implying that he despised and demeaned women. Trump loudly complained about Kelly until a truce was called. Later, the feud erupted again as Trump lambasted the network for what he called a pattern of unfair treatment. Then the network cancelled his appearance on *The O'Reilly Factor* when Trump announced a full-scale boycott of the network. The dispute reached its apex on Kelly's show, when *National Review* Editor Rich Lowry stated that Carly Fiorina had "cut (Trump's) balls off with the precision of a surgeon" in the second debate.

This foul language reportedly angered Fox News CEO Roger Ailes, who realized Trump had secured the moral high ground in the dispute. He offered to meet with Trump to discuss the type of coverage the front-runner was receiving on the network. In the end, no meeting occurred and a de facto truce was declared. While Trump appeared again on Fox News programs, he told Bill O'Reilly that he received better coverage on CNN.

Such coverage is understandable, since Fox News is the network that in previous elections promoted moderate Republican candidates over conservatives in the nomination contests. Thus George W. Bush, John McCain and Mitt Romney received much more favorable coverage on Fox News in their nomination battles against more conservative opponents.

In the current election cycle it is obvious that the majority of Fox commentators and guests are pulling for any candidate other than Donald Trump. First it was Jeb Bush, then Carly Fiorina, and eventually Marco Rubio. Conservative viewers understand this as well as Donald Trump does, and the only reason they stay loyal to the network is that the other choices are even worse.

The Trump Formula for Success

In late October, a Quinnipiac University poll showed that Dr. Ben Carson held a lead in Iowa; however, Donald Trump was still leading in every national poll on the GOP presidential race. Four months after he announced for president, Trump had defied the political professionals to claim the unquestioned lead.

Initially, the so-called experts had claimed his candidacy was just a publicity stunt, then they said Trump would implode from the weight of his controversial comments—yet nothing had stopped his ascension to the top of the Republican presidential field.

Despite ongoing battles with other candidates, and Fox News, and making a series of provocative statements, Trump stayed atop the GOP presidential polls for 94 days. Establishment reporters such as Chris Wallace of Fox News started to change their tune on Trump, stating that he "could be elected president of the United States."

At that point, a Rasmussen poll showed that Wallace was far from alone in this realization. Among likely Republican voters, 74% believed that Trump would be the party's nominee for president. This was an increase of 16% in just one week, showing that his campaign had entered a new, more serious phase.

Experts noted that Trump was getting better as a candidate, his answers sharper. Clearly, practice was making perfect. Trump conducted more media interviews and town hall meetings than any of his GOP opponents. He also offered more detailed plans on how to deal with national problems such as immigration, gun ownership and tax policy.

Trump accomplished all of this despite spending very little of his own money and refusing to accept major contributions. Amazingly, his campaign received $3.9 million in small, unsolicited contributions from 74,000 donors in the fall 2015 reporting period.

Although eventually even Trump was forced to spend some of his own money on the race, the amount was very little compared to establishment Republicans such as Jeb Bush who had spent millions carpet bombing the airwaves with negative advertisements in the early primary states. These establishment Republicans viewed Trump, a financially independent outsider, as the worst possible choice for the GOP nomination.

Fortunately, Trump was relatively immune to their attacks. Unlike any other presidential candidate in modern history, Trump was a successful businessman and reality TV star who was ratings gold for the cable news networks. It was no surprise that CNBC caved to his demand that their GOP presidential debate be limited to two hours. The network knew that with Trump on the debate stage they would have more viewers.

As evidence, with Trump participating in the first two GOP presidential candidate debates, the combined audience was 47.5 million viewers. The Democrats attracted only half as many viewers for their first two debates.

What is Trump's secret? Of course, he has had years of television training from his work on *The Apprentice* and as a media-savvy real estate tycoon. He is also an outsider in an election year in which voters are looking for a non-establishment politician to support.

But in addition to being the right type of candidate for this era in American politics, Trump possesses a certain skill set that sets him apart from the other candidates. According to Jim Crimmins, an international marketing communication specialist, Trump has a shrewd ability to dominate the political discussion. Crimmins believes that Trump drives the political debate, so the other candidates are always "reacting to what he says." In Crimmins' view, Trump "acts like a winner," and Americans feel it is time for their country to win again. He is creating a positive attitude among Americans, so more voters feel like voting for him.

In essence, Trump is not succeeding by making intellectual appeals; emotional appeals are the secret of his success. Americans realize that this country has been heading in the wrong direction for many years. Trump's campaign motto, "Make America Great Again," connects perfectly with millions of Americans who want to turn this country around.

Trump Overcomes Vicious Video Attack

By early November, a bevy of new polls showed Donald Trump and Dr. Ben Carson at the top of the GOP presidential race.

As one of the front runners, Trump faced a variety of mean-spirited attacks from fellow Republicans, Democrats, media commentators and liberal groups, including Hispanic advocacy organizations.

One of these groups, Deport Racism PAC, released a horrific video featuring young children spouting nasty profanity directed at Donald Trump. In the video, a young child named Ricardo directed his anger at Donald Trump, yelling "F—k you racist F—k." Other children featured in the video joined the profanity party by yelling obscenities at Trump and even giving him the middle finger salute.

The parents of the children involved in this video should be ashamed for their participation in an attack that was widely condemned by everyone from Hispanic activists to Trump's rival Senator Marco Rubio. It was truly despicable that the organization and video producer Luke Montgomery would have taken advantage of young children in such a disgusting manner. Political attacks would have been understandable, but when it involved abusing children, it obviously went way too far.

In response, Trump called the video a "disgrace" that "totally backfired." In fact, he stated that it led more Hispanic voters to support his campaign. Throughout his campaign, Trump has maintained that he "loves" Hispanic Americans and will help their community by bringing back jobs from countries such as India and China.

The video offensive was launched at Trump because he made stopping illegal immigration his signature campaign issue. Apart from calling for the deportation of illegal aliens and the construction of a wall, paid for by Mexico, along the southern border, he also noted that the influx of illegal immigrants from Mexico includes rapists and criminals. While this statement was politically incorrect, it was also undoubtedly true. In recent months, Americans had been horrified by the string of crimes committed by illegal aliens, including the July 1 murder of Kate Steinle in San Francisco.

Trump's tough talk on immigration was one of the major reasons why he raced to the top of the Republican polls. Yet this stance angered many leftists, including Montgomery and the supporters of the Deport Racism PAC. Montgomery contended that Trump's illegal immigration position was based on a view that Hispanics are "second class because they're brown." He justified the video of young children yelling obscenities as "using a bad word for a good cause."

In reality, Americans are tired of being told that protecting our borders is somehow racist. It is not racism to want our laws enforced. Once again, an attack against The Donald backfired; the net result of the video was more publicity for Trump and more support for his presidential campaign.

Republican Power Brokers Try to Steal the Nomination

With the Iowa caucuses getting closer and Donald Trump continuing to lead in the polls, the Republican Party power brokers began feeling desperate.

The GOP establishment was petrified by the notion of a Trump nomination, and was trying to devise a strategy to defeat him. On Monday, December 7, 2015, a group of moderate insiders met with Republican Party Chairman Reince Priebus and Senate Majority Leader Mitch McConnell to discuss the possibility of a brokered convention in Cleveland in July if Trump swept through the primaries with a delegate lead. The hope among the establishment was that moderates would unite behind a candidate like Jeb Bush to defeat Trump in a one-on-one matchup.

It was quite ironic that these political insiders were plotting a brokered convention since there had not been a dramatic Republican convention since the 1976 showdown in Kansas City between president Gerald Ford and conservative challenger Ronald Reagan. After Reagan's two terms, the establishment has controlled every nomination process until this one. Of course, the real reason for the meeting was that the establishment desperately wanted to defeat Trump. They despised the notion of a straight-talking, politically incorrect nominee who could not be controlled. As a billionaire, Trump did not need their money, a notion that truly frightened them. If Trump was nominated—or, heaven forbid, elected president—he could take away the power of the GOP establishment.

Trump is a very different kind of candidate, which upset GOP insiders like Priebus and McConnell. They were disgusted that Trump dominated discussion and news coverage. His call for a ban on Muslims entering the country only generated more media coverage for him. It also translated into more support among Republican voters.

In an early December CBS/New York Times poll, Trump led with 35% of the vote, more than double that of his nearest competitor, Senator Ted Cruz, who was at 16% support. Instead of derailing his campaign, the continual stream of supposed controversies only generated more support for Trump.

By the end of February 2016, Trump had won three contests, New Hampshire, South Carolina and Nevada, while Cruz had won Iowa. None of the more moderate candidates had won anything and several of them, such as Bush and Christie, had already exited the race.

The Donald certainly understands the unending plot to dethrone him as the frontrunner; that's why he's always said that he would remain in the GOP race as long as he was treated "fairly." He wants to keep the threat of leaving the Republican Party on the table, as an option.

According to a December 8, 2015 poll from *USA Today/Suffolk University*, if Trump ever did leave the GOP, 68% of his supporters would support him as an Independent presidential candidate. These results were no doubt disquieting for the Republican Party. Either they embraced Trump and allowed him to become the nominee, or rejected him and turned him toward a third party run that will likely kill the chances of the establishment's candidate.

The party elite also had to contend with another outsider, Dr. Ben Carson. By December, his poll numbers had dropped below Trump's, but he was still in the top tier of candidates. Like Trump, Carson was shunned by the party's establishment wing. Needless to say, Carson was furious when he learned of the secret meeting. "I will not sit by and watch a theft," he said. "I intend on being the nominee. If I am not, the winner will have my support. If the winner isn't our nominee, then we have a massive problem."

Ringside Politics Champion of the Year: Donald Trump

As mentioned previously, for many years we have bestowed a Ringside Politics Turkey of the Year Award to a worthy celebrity or politician. This designation is anything but flattering, so last year we decided to start a positive award category by recognizing an annual Champion of the Year.

The 2014 recipient was quite deserving: U.S. Senator Ted Cruz (R-TX). Ever since he burst upon the national stage, Cruz has stood up for conservative values in the midst of withering criticism. He has run a very efficient and effective presidential campaign and ended 2015 as unquestionably the candidate in second place in the national polls of Republican Party voters.

In 2015, the winner of the Ringside Politics Champion of the Year Award was the frontrunner in the GOP national polls: Donald Trump. Even though 2015 was a crazy year in American politics, it was dominated by Trump, who stole the spotlight from president Barack Obama.

Ever since he entered the presidential race in June, Trump captured the media headlines. All the other candidates have been forced to respond to his statements and his positions on the issues.

Fortunately, the public responded very favorably to Trump's politically incorrect message. While other politicians apologize on a regular basis for making controversial statements, Trump does the opposite; he doubles down.

Whether the issue was illegal aliens, the border wall, relations with Mexico, trade with China, Muslim immigration, or Hillary Clinton, Trump refused to play the normal political games and let the media dictate the conversation.

His rallies generated massive crowds and enthusiasm. Unlike other candidates, Trump was not scripted and actually took questions from the audience and the media. He was willing to go on all of the national political shows and, unlike Hillary Clinton, avoided none of them.

In one respect he won all five of the 2015 presidential debates, because his presence attracted massive viewership. The ratings for the GOP debates were spectacular due to one person, Donald Trump. On the other side, the Democrat presidential candidates drew only 8 million viewers to their second debate on ABC—a paltry one-third of the audience that watched of the first GOP debate on Fox News.

All this attention was due to the fact that Americans had never before seen a presidential candidate like Donald Trump. His track record of personal accomplishment is quite a contrast to that of most of his opponents, who are career politicians.

As a shrewd businessman, he operated a very unorthodox and streamlined campaign, spending very little money. Obviously, since Trump generated such massive media attention he did not need traditional advertising. After limited spending in 2015, he finally started to advertise more in January of 2016, spending some of his fortune to bolster his frontrunner status.

While most politicians are forced to spend precious time and energy raising funds, Trump has financed his entire campaign with little impact on his net worth. This gives Trump as major advantage over his opponents. Since he's not beholden to big donors, Trump is the ultimate independent candidate, obligated to no one except the voters who will determine whether he wins the presidential election or not.

A candidate who is not tied to special interests is a major threat to the Republican Party establishment, which of course is the reason party bigwigs tried to thwart his campaign. These GOP insiders and powerbrokers, who have nominated every Republican presidential candidate since Ronald Reagan, have no control over Trump.

It is very refreshing to see the elitists inside the Republican Party displaying such anxiety over the Trump campaign. Hopefully the Donald will continue to cause them heartburn, and his message of making America great again will continue to find strong support among Republican voters.

For all of these reasons and more, we were proud to present the 2015 Ringside Politics Champion of the Year Award to Donald Trump.

IX

2016
The GOP Evil Establishment
Strikes Back

By mid-January, front runner Donald Trump was in fighting form. In the 6ᵗʰ GOP presidential debate, he scored another strong performance. A Drudge Report poll showed 54% of respondents believed Trump won the debate, with Texas Senator Ted Cruz coming in second at 31%.

Most analysts believed it was Trump and Cruz who dominated the debate and maintained their position at the top of the polls. Clearly, neither candidate was a favorite of the dreaded GOP establishment, which was desperately trying to bolster the chances of a more moderate candidate to win the nomination. This is evil, because it is an attempt to thwart the will of the people and continue the power and privileges of a select few, the elite party insiders.

Their first choice, former Florida Governor Jeb Bush, was a total bust in the election. Bush languished in single digits, behind Trump, Cruz, Dr. Ben Carson and Florida Senator Marco Rubio.

To improve Bush's chances, additional endorsements started to flow in from moderates such as South Carolina Senator Lindsey Graham, who claimed that Bush was "ready to be a Commander-in-Chief on day one." Graham spent her career advocating a hawkish foreign policy with a call for more strident military action against enemies abroad. He claimed that Trump says things "that make no sense."

There was no love lost between Graham and Trump, who fired back at the Senator in a strongly worded Tweet, claiming that "Sen. Lindsey Graham embarrassed himself with his failed run for President and now further embarrasses himself with endorsement of Bush."

Bush hoped to make South Carolina his firewall, but to no avail. After a series of losses, his campaign was soon on life support. The establishment had a back-up plan if Bush faltered. The second choice was clearly Senator Marco Rubio, who was attractive to the party insiders because of his support for immigration reform. He was a member of the notorious "Gang of Eight," that tried to push through amnesty for illegal aliens. While Rubio struggled to connect with conservatives because of his pro-amnesty immigration position, the establishment clearly supported him.

If neither candidate gained traction against Trump, establishment Republicans had another option, block his nomination at the convention. In early December, a meeting was held to discuss the possibility of a brokered convention in Cleveland in July. A month later at the RNC meeting in Charleston, Holland Redfield, a committee member from the Virgin Islands, implored the party to stop Trump. Without mentioning his name, Redfield implied that Trump's position to block Muslim immigration and build a wall across the Southern border with Mexico was "reducing our label" and showing "disrespect in many cases for ethnic minorities." Redfield said he received plenty of support from other RNC members, who shared his dislike of Trump.

It was no surprise that the establishment agreed with Redfield. For example, South Carolina Governor Nikki Haley attacked Trump in the official Republican Party response to the President's State of the Union address. She said that the party should resist the "siren call of the angriest voices." She later admitted that it was "partially" aimed at Trump. Incredibly, her speech was approved by both House Speaker Paul Ryan and Senate Majority Leader Mitch McConnell, exposing to the nation the rift in the GOP.

All of these attacks showed that the Republican Party establishment was trying every possible method to take out Donald Trump, the party's presidential front runner. Of course, the Democrats would never do this, they are too smart to attempt intra party suicide.

Trump Causes Beltway Conservatives to go Crazy

By late January, Trump regained the lead in Iowa and continued to lead in the national polls. In the meantime, the media continued to obsess about everything Trump; his statements, his campaign and his rallies. As the candidate campaigned, his crowds were massive in Iowa, Oklahoma and Nevada.

On January 19, former Alaska Governor Sarah Palin, a Tea Party darling, enthusiastically endorsed Trump. This helped him among conservative and evangelical voters. He was also endorsed by the Duck Commander, Willie Robertson, who said that Trump was a "real leader" who epitomized "success and strength." Nonetheless, his critics did not stop their unrelenting attacks. Fox News host

Megyn Kelly gave plenty of air time to guests lambasting Trump as an inauthentic conservative.

On one program, Kelly continued her anti-Trump crusade by interviewing a panel of conservatives who penned anti-Trump columns for the *National Review* magazine. In fact, the magazine editors devoted their entire "Against Trump" edition to criticizing the Republican Party presidential front runner.

In true Trump fashion, he responded by labeling *National Review* as a "dying paper" and lamenting that the founder, "The late, great William F. Buckley would be ashamed of what had happened to his prize." It was remarkable to see a conservative magazine devote an entire issue to stopping one candidate. Never before had the magazine gone to such lengths to stop moderate Republicans like Gerald Ford, George H. W. Bush, Bob Dole, George W. Bush, John McCain, or Mitt Romney from winning the Republican nomination.

In fact, the *National Review* and Fox News and many others in the Beltway conservative media were very comfortable with a "neo-con," or moderate winning the nomination. With Trump, there is incredible discomfort for he is a very different type of Republican presidential candidate. Unfortunately for Kelly and other media critics, their attacks just made Trump supporters more committed and angrier at the media.

Unlike the other candidates, Trump self-financed his campaign, so no donors had any influence over him. If elected President, he will not be controlled by GOP power brokers on special interest influence peddlers. Thus, he is hated by the right people, namely the Republican establishment.

In contrast, conservative hero Senator Ted Cruz received $12 million in Wall Street donations, second only to Jeb Bush among Republican presidential candidates. Cruz also failed to reveal during his 2012 U.S. Senate campaign that he received loans totaling $1 million from Goldman Sachs and CitiBank. While Cruz claimed it was a "paperwork error," others believed he was trying to hide his Wall Street ties.

Cruz ran on a very conservative platform, but he rarely discussed his work as campaign legal adviser and later Deputy Attorney General in the George W. Bush administration. It was Cruz who recruited future Supreme Court Justice John Roberts to the Bush legal team during the 2000 Florida presidential recount fight. His wife, Heidi Cruz, also worked in the Bush administration as an economic and national security adviser before joining the Wall Street firm Goldman Sachs.

Obviously, Cruz was not that much of an outsider. The real outsider was Donald Trump and that upset many Beltway conservatives. Unlike the other GOP presidential candidates, Trump is extremely strong on the issue of border security. He was the first to champion a border wall and claim that Mexico will pay for it. He wants to deport the illegal immigrants and stop Muslim immigration into the country. This is not popular with many leaders in the Republican Party who are in favor of open borders and want the cheap labor of illegal immigrants. They are controlled by crony capitalists who have benefited nicely from traditional Republican leadership, but would suffer greatly if Trump is elected President.

On other issues such as trade, Trump presents a nationalist stance that is steadfastly against the United States running massive deficits with countries such as China and Japan. Many so-called conservative leaders are in favor of phony "free trade" and have no problems with the United States running massive deficits. They support the Trans Pacific Partnership, a colossal international trade deal that is an attack on U.S sovereignty. Cruz initially supported the trade deal, and then flipped his position as he has done on a number of other issues, including amnesty for illegal aliens.

By late January 2016, the conservative movement was split with many supporting Trump and others supporting Cruz, despite his Wall Street ties and inconsistent positions on key issues. Trump was the more popular choice because of his non-political background and his ability to expand the Republican coalition. For the first time in decades, the GOP was attracting working class voters, Reagan Democrats, to support Trump. As evidence, it was clear to see hard working Americans and a cross-section of all socio-economic classes attending the raucous Trump rallies. This type of varied and enthusiastic support was the type any candidate would need to win a presidential election.

While Cruz still had to worry about a lawsuit challenging his eligibility for the presidential campaign as a "natural born citizen," and the potential of answering a judicial call to action, Trump has to answer to no one, but the people of America.

The Big Bush Bust

The results from Iowa were certainly interesting. On the Democratic side, Hillary Clinton and Bernie Sanders virtually tied, giving both campaigns some momentum going into New Hampshire. Whereas, the laughable, struggling Martin O'Malley finally decided to end his ridiculous campaign after getting less than 1% of the vote in Iowa.

On the Republican side, former Arkansas Governor Mike Huckabee ended his campaign after failing to recapture the magic of 2008 and pull off a miracle upset in Iowa. After a poor finish, at least he had the good sense to quit. The same can't be said for former Florida Governor Jeb Bush, who finished a pathetic sixth place among Republican voters, yet vowed to continue the fight in New Hampshire and beyond.

In 2015, Bush was the overwhelming favorite to win the nomination. He is part of the Bush dynasty as his father and brother served as President, so he had a tremendous built-in advantage. He enjoyed easy access to the wealthy, establishment donors who control the Republican Party. These power brokers flooded his campaign with massive donations, allowing Bush to establish the early lead in the polls and in the important category of fundraising.

It soon evaporated as Bush tangled with Donald Trump in the debates and was labeled both stiff and "low energy." Throughout the campaign, Bush failed to connect with Republican voters looking for action on the important issues of the economy, illegal immigration and the fight against ISIS. The end result was his uninspiring performance in Iowa, where he finished with only 2.8% of the vote.

In fact, Bush wasted almost $15 million in Iowa to garner just 5,165 votes, spending as astronomical $2,884 per Iowa vote.

His horrible showing reflected the desire of Republican voters to move past the Bush family and find new leadership in the party. Voters realized that Jeb Bush was a creature of the much despised Republican establishment and, if elected, would not do anything to fix the real problems facing the nation.

Bush's anemic level of support was the best result of the Iowa election. It placed his campaign on life support going to New Hampshire and made his nomination very unlikely. Of course, this was all bad news for the Democrats who were looking to coast to victory in November if the Republicans nominated another Bush.

With the top three Republican candidates in Iowa being Cruz, Trump and Rubio, voters sent an unmistakable message to the GOP establishment that it was time for new leadership. It was also the only possible way for Republicans to have a chance of recapturing the White House in November of 2016.

The Perils of Papal Politics

Pope Francis is a man of great compassion and humility. He shows tremendous concern for the young, the elderly and the sick. He advocates for those who have been forgotten, such as the homeless. He has shunned the luxuries and trappings of his position and performs his duties in a much more modest style than his predecessors. These are admirable qualities and set a good example for all Catholics.

While there is much to like about Pope Francis, there is much to be concerned about. When he starts discussing climate change, immigration or economics, his comments seem based more on leftist ideology than reality.

After concluding a trip to Mexico on February 18, the Pope entertained questions from reporters. Not surprisingly, he was asked about Donald Trump's plan, if elected President, to build a wall on the Mexican border and deport illegal immigrants. Sadly, the Pope made offensive comments regarding Trump and, instead of refraining from entering the political debate in this country, jumped right in.

He said, "A person who thinks only about building walls, wherever they may be, and not of building bridges, is not Christian. This is not the Gospel. As far as what you said about whether I would advise to vote or not to vote, I am not getting involved in that. I say only this man is not Christian if he has said things like that."

In true Trump fashion, he responded and called the comments "disgraceful." He noted that if ISIS attacks the Vatican, "I can promise you that the pope would have only wished and prayed that Donald Trump would have been president, because this would not have happened."

It is quite ironic that the Pope, who is protected by massive walls at the Vatican, criticized a presidential candidate who is calling for similar protection in this country. In fact, the Pope's response reflects mind boggling hypocrisy.

Of course, in his shocking comments, the Pope not only defamed Trump, but also the millions of Americans who share his views. A growing number of Americans are disgusted with the lack of border enforcement. They are tired of illegal aliens receiving benefits and taking jobs from law abiding Americans.

Hopefully, the Pope was just misinformed about this real crisis impacting America and did not understand the extent of the crime and illegal drugs crossing the border. During his tenure, the Pope has advocated for more illegal immigrants to be accepted in the United States. Yet, as Trump noted, the Pope does not realize that with illegal immigration comes "the crime, the drug trafficking and the negative economic impact" on the United States.

These comments continue a trend of liberal activism that has been apparent during the tenure of Pope Francis. Along with calling for open borders and immigration and forceful action on climate change, he has repeatedly criticized capitalism. This simplistic view overlooks the extent of human misery caused by socialism and communism, which is rampant in the Pope's homeland, Argentina, and many other countries in Latin America.

It would have been more appropriate for Pope Francis to direct his barbs at the real tyrants of this region, such as Raul and Fidel Castro. Yet, when the Pope visited Cuba, he warmly embraced Castro, overlooking his history of political repression and his antagonism against religion. Along with murdering priests, Castro has shuttered religious schools and oppressed believers of all faiths.

Instead of lambasting Castro and the other socialist tyrants of Latin America, Pope Francis focused his rhetorical fire on Donald

Trump, an advocate of capitalism who wants to enhance our national security.

In this case, it was more than just criticism of Trump's positions on the issues; the Pope also called into question, his Christianity. This attack gave Trump the invitation to respond and defend his faith. He said, "I am proud to be a Christian and as President I will not allow Christianity to be consistently attacked and weakened, unlike what is happening now, with our current President. No leader, especially a religious leader, should have the right to question another man's religion or faith."

The Vatican later clarified the Pope's comments and said it was "not a personal attack."

In the future, a better approach for the Pope would be to forgo the politics and focus on saving souls and preaching the Gospel. Heaven knows that the world needs that mission more than another religious leader playing the role of a liberal politician.

The Disgraceful New York Times

On February 23, Ross Douthat, a columnist for the *New York Times*, set a new low for his liberal publication. As a supposed joke, Douthat tweeted that the best way to stop Donald Trump was to attempt to assassinate him. He said, "Good news, I've figured out how the Trump campaign ends," and included a link to a scene from the 1983 movie, "The Dead Zone," which featured an attempted assassination attempt on a deranged political candidate who had visions of running for President.

This was both disgusting and outrageous, even for the *New York Times*. If such a threat had been made against President Obama, the reporter would have been arrested and faced charges. If such a threat had been made against Hillary Clinton, the reporter would have been immediately fired and been the subject of nationwide ridicule. However, since the victim of this reprehensible attack was Donald Trump, the *New York Times* did absolutely nothing. In fact, it seems that Douthat was not even reprimanded by the newspaper.

Of course, reporters have the right of free speech and we live in a country with a free press and cherish the First Amendment. However, news organizations should also have standards and advocating violence against a public figure should be unacceptable behavior.

After the initial tweet caused an intensely negative reaction from Trump supporters, Douthat apologized and removed the offensive comment. Nevertheless, the damage had already been done. Trump is a very controversial presidential candidate that has Secret Service protection. He reportedly faces death threats on a regular basis. According to his former aide, Roger Stone, Trump wears a bullet proof vest for protection.

The tweet may have given lunatics the encouragement to attempt to harm Trump, who has spent the campaign in front of large crowds. Thanks to the lowlife columnist, the already difficult job of the Secret Service was made even more difficult.

Since his presidential campaign began in June of 2015, Trump dealt with public threats against his life a number of times. In October, a notorious Mexican drug lord, El Chapo, reportedly put a $100 million bounty on Trump's head. In December, when Trump called for a halt on Muslim immigration into this country, the Internet exploded with death threats against him.

Of course, it is not unusual for drug lords and terrorists to target U.S. presidential candidates, but it is unprecedented for a *New York Times* columnist to join the fray.

Mitt Romney is the Darth Vader for the Evil Empire

On March 3, at a speech in Salt Lake City, 2012 Republican Party presidential nominee and former Massachusetts Governor Mitt Romney laid out his reasons why Donald Trump should never receive the Republican endorsement. According to Romney, Trump is a "phony" and a "fraud," who would lose to Hillary Clinton in the fall election.

Romney favored a deadlocked GOP presidential race that withholds the nomination from Trump at the convention. It was only the latest in a series of desperate attacks launched by Republican Establishment that was routed by Trump in 10 of the first 15 states to hold elections.

The establishment viewed Trump as a wild card, a loose cannon. They could not control a candidate who self-funded his presidential campaign. Trump also opposed the Republican Establishment on fundamental issues such as amnesty for illegal aliens and the Trans Pacific Partnership.

While Romney was hyper critical of Trump, he was more than happy to receive the businessman's endorsement in the 2012 presidential race. In fact, he appeared with Trump at a news conference and asked Trump to record phone calls for his campaign in six states. In fact, Trump said that Romney would have been happy to "drop to his knees" to receive his endorsement.

Why the change of heart? Romney and his friends in the GOP establishment realized that Trump was a real threat to win the party's nomination and they were willing to destroy their White House chances to prevent that from happening.

With Trump at the helm of the Republican Party, the

establishment would be finished. Their cozy relationships with lobbyists, special interest groups and the politicians on Capitol Hill would be destroyed.

To save the day for the evil establishment empire, they found their Darth Vader, Mitt Romney. The arrogance displayed in his speech was stunning. No Republican should care what he said about anything. Romney is a three time losing political candidate, who ran a horrible presidential campaign against Barack Obama in 2012. In the last two debates, Romney was neutered and ineffective. He refused to run an aggressive campaign against a heavily damaged Obama and lost a race that clearly he should have won. So, clearly Mitt Romney had no standing to lecture anyone about the 2016 presidential race.

Romney's antagonism against Trump was similar to the scorched earth campaign he ran against Newt Gingrich in the 2012 Florida Republican primary. Gingrich was overwhelmed by a barrage of nasty, inaccurate commercials that ran almost non-stop on statewide television. It was a multi-million-dollar campaign of political personal destruction. This was what the GOP establishment planned for Trump during the rest of the GOP race.

This sordid history showed that Romney and the Republican Party establishment cared more about denying a conservative outsider the nomination than winning the presidency.

By blasting Trump, Romney and his establishment cronies, in essence, expressed criticism for the millions of Americans who supported the New York businessman. On Super Tuesday alone, Trump received approximately 3 million votes. Romney and his elitist party snobs were outraged that so many Americans are so concerned about the border, trade, jobs and putting this country first.

It was Trump's populist and nationalist messages that were

anathema to the globalist, free trade, big government Republican Party elite. They hated the fact that so many Americans were concerned about these issues and wanted the borders secure, manufacturing jobs to return to this country and the trade deficit lowered.

Romney's attack was just a foreshadowing of the relentless stream of Trump bashing that occurred in the months following his speech. For example, Romney, the 2012 nominee, was soon joined by 2008 GOP presidential nominee, Arizona Senator John McCain, who called Trump "dangerous."

The ultimate goal of Romney and the Republican establishment was to force a brokered convention in July in which Trump would not have enough delegates for the nomination on the first ballot and then delegates will be pressured to abandon Trump on the second ballot and select a compromise nominee like Romney or Speaker of the House Paul Ryan.

Such a harebrained idea was never workable and, if enacted, would have destroyed the GOP's White House hopes. It would have forced Trump voters, if not Trump himself, to abandon the party in massive numbers. Sadly, the party elite did not care for they are quite comfortable losing the White House to the Democrats again, as long as they retain their party positions and power.

They much preferred Hillary Clinton, a scandal ridden liberal, to Donald Trump, the candidate with the most support on the Republican side who enticed millions of new people to the party. In a world turned upside down, Mitt Romney and the Republican Party leadership tried to annihilate their leading candidate who generated the most delegates and by far the most votes. Only the Republican Party could be so stupid.

Republican Elite Determined to Elect Hillary

By late March, the hysteria coming from GOP conservative purists and party insiders about Donald Trump reached ridiculous proportions. Talk show host Glenn Beck compared the Republican frontrunner to Hitler, while Nebraska Senator Ben Sasse thundered that he will never support Trump if he is the nominee.

The problem for these Trump haters was that the front runner had garnered an impressive 7.5 million votes to date; along with 679 delegates and won 19 states, more than double the number for his nearest competitor, Texas Senator Ted Cruz. He was clearly energizing Americans across the country and winning in every region of the country.

In the process, he was bringing in new voters who had not supported a Republican candidate in decades. The old "Reagan Democrat" coalition of blue collar, working class and union members were seeing Donald Trump as a champion for their values and a candidate with an answer to their ever growing economic woes.

The problem was that the elite of both parties were perfectly comfortable relegating millions of working class Americans to the dustbin of history. In this campaign, Trump attracted these voters with his demand to stop illegal immigration, horrible trade deals, corporations abandoning America and millions of jobs being shipped overseas.

As a result of this message, Trump's support had been growing ever since he entered the race in June. Not only Republicans, but Democrats and Independents favorably responded to both his message and his politically incorrect style. Despite being a first time candidate, he defied convention wisdom and withstood withering criticism and vicious attacks to unquestionably lead the GOP race for the nomination.

This development did not sit well with the establishment in both the Republican Party and the conservative movement. To say there was uproar among the elites is an understatement. Many of these so-called leaders claimed they would never support Trump if he became the nominee.

On March 17, a group convened by Republican blogger and commentator Eric Erickson met in Washington D.C. in a desperate move to stop Donald Trump from securing the GOP presidential nomination. This effort did not impress former House Speaker and presidential candidate Newt Gingrich, who said that the group, "ought to at least be honest and say to people, 'You know, I'd rather have Hillary Clinton than the Republican nominee,' because that's what they're doing. They ought to just form 'Lost Republicans for Hillary' and be honest about the effect of what they're doing."

Of course Newt was right. By trying to stop Trump, these conservative purists were in effect helping Hillary. Trump also threatened the elite's cozy relationships, high priced contracts and insider deals. He does not need their money and, if elected, will walk into the White House owing no one. As President, he would be able to truly act for the American people instead of the special interests. It has been decades since the American people have had a truly independent President.

As President, Trump will not owe any foreign governments either. The countries that depend on U.S. economic and military aid are apoplectic as Trump threatens this "world order."

All of this potential change was just too much for House Speaker Paul Ryan (R-WI), who has been a total disappointment to conservatives. Ryan was clearly hoping for a contested convention. He said that none of the remaining contenders will be able to secure the nomination and predicted that a contested convention could "very well become a reality." Obviously, his abilities as a prognosticator were as good as his abilities as a conservative bulwark against Obama liberalism.

Ryan claimed that he was not offering himself as a potential GOP presidential nominee and "unity" candidate; however, that idea was floated by former House Speaker John Boehner. Another possibility, of course was 2012 GOP presidential nominee Mitt Romney who made headlines with strong denunciations of Trump. Romney was another darling of the establishment, but he had the baggage of being a three-time political loser.

Among the two remaining Trump opponents, Ohio Governor John Kasich tried to position himself as the establishment alternative if the convention was brokered. Most of the GOP delegates were bound to support their candidate on the first ballot, but may switch support on a second ballot.

The other candidate, U.S. Senator Ted Cruz, also lined up some establishment support with endorsements from U.S. Senator Lindsey Graham (R-SC), Jeb Bush and his brother Neil, former Texas Governor Rick Perry among others. While Cruz did well with party leaders, he was not able to match Trump's success at the ballot box. According to Gingrich, Trump was an "unusual phenomenon," who "mastered popular communication," and if elected President "would be an absolute outlier in the trajectory of American politics."

With 19 trillion in debt, 94 million Americans outside of the workforce, a growing trade deficit, a wide open border, 15.7 million illegal immigrants, a struggling war against Islamic terrorism and anxiety throughout the country, it was time for "an absolute outlier" to be elected President.

Despite wailing and crying from elites, the bottom line was that Trump received millions of votes more than another other Republican candidate. He was the choice of the people. As noted by Florida Governor Rick Scott, "Donald Trump is the will of the people. We need to listen to the people, back his candidacy and win in November."

The consultants, experts, analysts, party bosses and purists did not get anything right in the 2016 Republican presidential race. What they continued to overlook was the stunning popularity of Donald Trump, who withstood tens of millions of dollars in attack ads and prevailed against 16 experienced opponents.

These critics should have realized that someone with such broad and loyal support deserved the nomination, with a real chance of being elected President. Unfortunately, the sad, but disturbing, truth is that many in the Republican Party leadership would much prefer President Hillary Clinton to President Donald Trump.

Michelle Fields Dreams of her Fifteen Minutes of Fame

After his loss in Wisconsin on April 5, Trump regained his footing in the race for President. He generated national outrage over the tactics of the Colorado Republican Party, which canceled a "planned vote" and "sidelined" one million GOP voters. After a state convention, Colorado awarded all of their 34 delegates to Senator Ted Cruz.

Trump called foul and many Americans agreed with his complaint. It was one reason that a Fox News national poll showed Trump leading Cruz 45-27%, a very healthy margin. In the New York primary on April 19, Trump destroyed Cruz and Kasich, winning over 60% of the vote. The following week, he swept all five Northeastern states with massive margins over his opponents. He extended his delegate lead to 300+ over Cruz.

Another development which helped Trump was the decision by Palm Beach County State Attorney David Kronberg not to prosecute Trump campaign manager Corey Lewandowski for battery of reporter Michelle Fields.

Police charged Lewandowski with the battery of Fields, who claimed that the Trump campaign manager yanked her arm and bruised her after a Trump event in March.

The entire case was a ridiculous joke as a video showed Lewandowski barely touched Fields and did not injure her. Lewandowski was protecting his candidate after a campaign event. At the event, Fields disregarded Secret Service instructions and placed herself right next to the candidate. Lewandowski did not know her, neither did Trump. In his mind, she might not have been a reporter, but someone trying to harm his candidate. Lewandowski had no idea, so he was doing his job as a campaign manager to protect his candidate, who received multiple death threats over the course of the campaign.

Clearly, the entire incident was an attempt by Fields to create attention and garner publicity. After the episode was initially reported, she resigned from Breitbart News, claiming that the website editors did not show enough support for her. Thereafter, she was given plenty of free air time by Megyn Kelly of Fox News and others in the media who hate Trump and want to publicize anything that will harm his campaign.

The problem was that there was scant evidence to support Fields and the battery charge. Initially, Fields claimed to have been yanked so hard that she "almost fell to the ground." The video showed no such encounter.

In the aftermath of the case being dismissed, Fields reportedly was considering filing a defamation lawsuit against Lewandowski and Trump. If the suit is eventually filed, it will make her look like an obsessed reporter trying to cling to her 15 minutes of fame. If the suit is filed, it will garner attention, but will likely fail. In the eyes of the public, such a move will make Trump and Lewandowski look like the targets of a publicity seeking reporter.

In the aftermath of the Palm Beach announcement, Lewandowski praised Trump in a CNN interview for his "loyalty," and said that "a lesser person, another politician, would have terminated me on the spot." In the interview, Lewandowski claimed that prior to the incident, which only lasted "three seconds," he had never met Fields. After hearing on social media that Fields was upset, Lewandowski called Fields, but she never returned his call.

Clearly, she was not interested in making peace with Lewandowski, instead she was interested in making this so called incident a big story. Maybe it was an attempt to boost her career or an attempt to embarrass Trump, but, while it worked initially, in the end, she was the one who looked ridiculous.

Lewandowski said that Fields wanted to "inject herself into making it a story." She succeeded in that regard, but it was at the expense of her reputation as a serious and objective reporter.

Trump vs. Clinton

When Trump decisively won the Indiana primary on May 3 with 53% of the vote, both Cruz and Kasich called it quits, suspending their campaigns. The first time candidate outlasted all of the veteran politicians, the attack ads, the party naysayers and the best efforts of the GOP establishment. It was truly a historic victory for Donald Trump and his millions of supporters. By the end of the 2016 race, Trump will break all records for total number of votes in a Republican Party presidential nomination race.

Trump won decisively despite spending very little of his own money and using the media to his advantage. Throughout the GOP nomination battle, Trump controlled the narrative and drove the media coverage. The other candidates were exasperated, demoralized and outfoxed by a media veteran who had been a household name for decades as a real estate mogul and a reality television star.

In an ironic twist, despite the predictions of the so-called experts of a contested or brokered convention, the Republican presidential race was over after the Indiana primary with Trump as the clear cut winner. In contrast, the battle continued among Democrats with Senator Bernie Sanders refusing to go away. In a surprise, he won the Indiana primary by a comfortable 5% margin over Hillary Clinton. Once again, Sanders exposed the weakness of Hillary Clinton, the scandal ridden former Secretary of State with the poor communication and political skills. All the excitement on the Democrat side rested with Sanders who captured the support of younger voters and those disgusted with the party establishment.

Despite the Senator's win in Indiana and the possibility of victories in other states, the stage is set for Clinton to win the nomination. In fact, the Democrat Party establishment proved to be more powerful than the GOP establishment, who were unable to stop Trump. Eventually, Clinton will capture the nomination due to her strong support among super delegates, hundreds of party leaders who have committed to her campaign. The deck was literally stacked against Sanders from the beginning, giving him very little chance of ever winning the nomination.

Thus, the 2016 general election contest will pit two universally known candidates against each other. The race between Donald Trump vs. Hillary Clinton will be an election for the ages. If elected, Trump will represent the country's best chance of moving in a new direction, while a Clinton presidency will deliver another four years of the Obama agenda. If he follows through on his promises, a

President Trump will build a wall and secure the southern border, stop illegal immigration, temporarily halt Muslim immigration, repeal and replace Obamacare, reduce personal and corporate taxes, end bad trade deals, bring home jobs from overseas, rebuild the military and destroy ISIS. Under President Hillary Clinton, the country will see higher deficits, more government spending, a weakening of our military, a growing terrorist threat, open borders, unchecked illegal immigration, an expansion of socialized medicine and higher taxes. As a Clinton, she will also reintroduce scandal and corruption back into the White House.

There will be tremendous voter interest in the election and the ratings for the televised debates will break viewership records. It will be the most important election in our country's history with the future of America at stake. The country may not survive a Hillary Clinton presidency, so hopefully we will be spared that potentially catastrophic experience.

CONCLUSION

The battle for control of the Republican Party has been ongoing for decades; however, it has been especially intense over the last few years, the time period chronicled in this book. On the one side are the party bosses and insiders, and on the other side are the grassroots conservatives. Usually the party leadership battles and presidential nominations are won by the more moderate establishment wing of the party, which has all the advantages in terms of funding, endorsements and publicity.

For this reason, in the years since Ronald Reagan's remarkable run, every Republican presidential nomination has been won by a moderate. However, the tide turned in the 2016 presidential race: as the top two candidates were outsiders, disliked by party leaders.

In their fierce battle for the nomination, both Donald Trump and Ted Cruz provided a tremendous service to the GOP by challenging the corrupt alliance of special interests, party leaders, political consultants and the national news media.

These candidates went around, above and through the forces arrayed against them. Trump and Cruz connected with the one group of people often forgotten by these Beltway snobs; the Republican voters, the average people who are disgusted by what is happening in their country and furious that the Republican Party is not doing anything to change it.

After years of this ineffective GOP leadership, the 2016 election proved to be the time that the Republican Party finally returned to its grassroots and the conservative principles outlined in its platform. With the nomination of Donald Trump, it was the year the Republican establishment was finally defeated.

It remains to be seen whether Trump can defeat Hillary Clinton, and bring conservative values back to the White House. However, at least as a fighting conservative he will have a chance to defeat her. Only a Trump victory will provide our country the opportunity to recover from the incredible damage of the Obama years. A President Hillary Clinton could be the death knell of this country.

The stakes for a presidential election have never been higher. This political revolution must succeed. If not, the prospects for our beloved country are very bleak. In this election, it is imperative that all Republicans unite behind Donald Trump and his conservative agenda. Once that occurs, the Republican Party will reclaim the White House, and, most importantly, our country will be saved.

JEFF CROUERE is the former Executive Director and Deputy Chairman of the Louisiana Republican Party and the founder of the Northshore Tea Party, the largest group in the state. Since 1999, he has hosted Ringside Politics, a radio and TV show which examines controversial current events.

A TV political analyst, a columnist for selected publications and websites and the host of Politics with a Punch, a political comedy show starring a panel of celebrities, Crouere has moderated forums featuring statewide and presidential candidates and been interviewed for his expertise on Fox News, CNN and other cable networks.

For speaking engagements and media appearances, Jeff Crouere can be contacted at #504-669-6076 or jcrouere@gmail.com

Visit his website www.RingsidePolitics.com for more information about his programs; follow him at www.Facebook.com/ RingsidePolitics or on Twitter:@jeffcrouere